everything a girl

to know about...

football

SIMEON DE LA TORRE • SOPHIE BROWN

A & C BLACK • LONDON

Published in 2005 by A & C Black (Publishers) Ltd
37 Soho Square, London W1D 3QZ
www.acblack.com

ISBN 0 7136 7241 2

A CIP catalogue record for this book is available from the British Library.

Typeset by Palimpsest Book Production Limited, Polmont, Stirlingshire

Printed in Great Britain by Bookmarque Ltd, Croydon, Surrey

Contents

Acknowledgements

Simeon would like to thank Clare for convincing him that there was a real need for this book by persistently talking throughout crucial goal replays on the television – and for her support, patience and love, naturally. He would also like to thank his co-author Sophie for her enthusiasm and for her guidance when it came to the intricate inner workings of the female mind. Adam Burns, Mike Peake and Ed Halliwell are the three publishing powerhouses that gave him a break in the murky world of magazines, and to all his other commissioning editors he says: 'Ta. Oh, and I'm free next week if you've got any work on...' He would like to thank Sofia and Evie for keeping the noise down when he was writing the book from home, and finally he would like to extend his gratitude to the Spain football team, Real Madrid and Bristol City for providing him with years of frustration, unrivalled entertainment, and periods of abject misery respectively.

Sophie would like to thank her mum for making her realise that the state of Michael Owen's knees was something that she really should be worrying about, and also 'The Girls' – especially Tanya, Anna, Emma and Lyn – for making her realise she was not alone in her biological misunderstanding of the great game. Sophie would also like to say thank you to her co-author Simeon for having the foresight to see the potential of this book and for bringing it to life with his hilarious prose. To Greenock Morton Football Club, for introducing her to more colourful language than she had ever heard before, Spurs fans for not beating her up when she went to live games and all the pub bores who have tried and failed to explain the offside rule. And finally to Paul, her husband to be, for his love, support and enduring patience – particularly during matches, when she repeatedly asks him which end her team's goal is. She hopes this book will help ease the pain of Sunday afternoon Sky Sports sessions throughout married life.

The authors would both like to thank their editor Hannah McEwen, Bill Brown for his wonderful illustrations, and all of the team at A&C Black.

Introduction

Men aren't complex beasts, they only care about a handful of things: football, sex, drink, food and 'having a laugh' – and if they can successfully combine two of those ingredients at any one time, they're happy. Women have known for years that the way to a man's heart is through his stomach and the same is true of his favourite game. But getting to grips with football isn't just about pulling or keeping a man, it's about genuinely enjoying the world's most popular sport with the same passion, excitement and enthusiasm as everyone else. Because there must be something in it, mustn't there?

You can blame Paul Gascoigne. It's his fault that the nation is obsessed by football. Before the Tyneside wonder wept during the England versus Germany match in the 1990 World Cup, most of the population regarded football as a game played by fat, puffing dads (with names like Norman 'Bites Yer Legs' Hunter) in grim stadiums in front of gritty working men who liked to smoke things that smelt like bicycle inner tubes stuffed with tar.

Almost overnight, Gazza's tears changed all that. Retrospectively, things might have been a little different if we'd known just how highly strung (read: mentally unhinged) he was in the first place, but the (foot)ball was already rolling. The England team had done well in a major competition, several members of the squad became household names and, before you knew it, the public in general were looking forward to the new domestic season, which was just a few short weeks away. The fat dads' days were numbered.

Since then, of course, the game and the fans have changed almost beyond recognition. Well, perhaps not that much – the same rules apply and the fans haven't mutated into a different species or anything – but the whole sport is that much more glossy, sparkly and, er, sexy. The First Division was renamed The Premier League; Sky bought the television rights to the game and gave us swooshy graphics and razzmatazz; the ageing, overweight players were replaced by younger, fitter and, it has to be said, much better looking ones; footballers' haircuts in general got *so* much better; and hot beefy drinks and meat pies were replaced on the terrace menus by caffé lattes and salmon wraps. Actually, that last bit isn't strictly true – the reconstituted meat products remain.

Nevertheless, it's easy to see why so many more women are watching the game today than ever before. An interview with the England Captain David Beckham will sell far more copies in a women's glossy magazine than in a boys' soccer comic.

Trouble is, there are plenty of people – male supporters, mainly – within the footballing fraternity who don't want to welcome new female fans into the sport. Or at least that's the impression they give. Mention at work that you watched a game at the weekend and you'll face a barrage of questions from the Office Footie Nut designed to test your depth of love and knowledge of the game. What you might really want to say is: 'Look, I don't know who came on for Fox or if they played a sweeper system. All I know is that we lost 2–1, I had a good night out and was eyed up by about 100 men, which was a result in itself,' but that won't wash with blokes; they want facts and stats before they'll welcome you into their innermost world. Granted, it's a mad world full of ancient results, images of grown men in shorts hugging each other, league tables and slow-motion replays, but to gain access to this universe is as close to intimacy with some blokes as you're gonna get.

Unfortunately, some have lost sight of the fact that football is just a bit of theatre where 22 men chase a leather ball around a pitch for our entertainment. There's a famous quote by former Liverpool manager Bill Shankly: 'Some people believe football is a matter of life and death. I can assure you it is much, much more important than that.' A pithy speech indeed, but the sentiment behind it is comparable to a Greek waiter telling you he loves you. Yet it explains the level of passion that football elicits from some of its followers.

However, you *do* need football in your life. Not just to help you pull a man or get closer to the one you've already got, but because sometimes, just sometimes, it's better than sex. And it's often better than chocolate. Yes, there'll be times when you'll feel humiliated, ashamed and just plain dirty – but sex can be like that too. Being there when your team scores the winning goal in the final of a major competition is like experiencing a glorious, screaming public orgasm. Even just the build up to a World Cup Finals or a European

Championships can be as exquisite as flirting with an old flame. But to fully appreciate the game, the build up and even the post-match analysis, it's much better to get to grips with the rules, lingo, etiquette and nuances of the sport – and it's not as hard as you might think.

Most men are schooled in football from their early years – why, most new dads can't wait to buy their son their first kit and can often be heard coming out with nonsense such as: 'he may be only two, but I've a feeling he's going to play for his country one day.' Even if the dads themselves are rubbish at playing. These dads will then give their daughters a tea set and mutter something about 'making someone a lovely wife one day.' Puh!

If you're the type of girl who could nip to the loo and walk in front of the big screen in the pub in the 89th minute of a game – without realising that you've done anything wrong – then this is the book for you. If you quite enjoy it when the Champions' League is on the telly but you can't get your

head around aggregate scoring, you've come to the right place. If you want to find out what the devil the commentators are on about when they come out with phrases such as 'onion bag' and 'row z', this crash-course can help.

And if you want to wipe the smug smirk off the face of that Office Footie Nut come Monday morning, you just need to read on...

1

Pick 11 men to share the rest of your life with...

the teams

Whereas players can defect to rival clubs at the drop of a cheque, supporters can *never ever** change their allegiance to a team once publicly declared. In fact, being seen cheering for any other club than the one you once mentioned in passing to a casual acquaintance carries a social stigma akin to sleeping with a first cousin. Both are

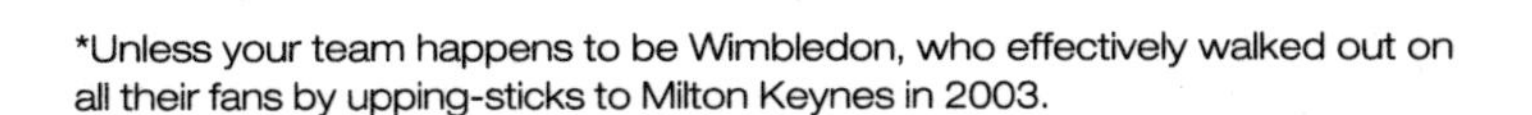

*Unless your team happens to be Wimbledon, who effectively walked out on all their fans by upping-sticks to Milton Keynes in 2003.

perfectly legal, but both are equally likely to drive your dad to drink.

It's an unlikely scenario, but even if your boys were to go down four seasons in a row and end up playing part-time football in a cattle shed while the team up the road took on five of the most gorgeous and gifted players on the planet and splashed out on a new kit that 'does things' for you, you'd still be morally obliged to follow your original team. The reason? Well, without getting too touchy-feely about it, supporters are the beating heart of a club. The players will kick a ball for anyone who'll keep them in designer lager, managers come and go, the board are more concerned with making money and the staff certainly don't work for the love of it. Which leaves the fans. And what would happen if everyone got seduced by the scandalously tight shorts of the team up the road...?

choosing a team

If you've never declared an affinity for any particular club, you can betroth yourself to any team for pretty much any reason whatsoever:

- You fancy one (or more) of the players
- They're winners
- They've got a nice kit
- Your fella supports them
- Your ex-boyf supported their rivals.

Granted, the above reasons may seem a little inane, but rest assured that many, many hardened fans have chosen their teams on the strength of the same criteria. Sure, a man may tell you he supports a club from miles away because his father followed them for decades, but it's just as likely that as a lad he quite liked the look of their stripy shirts or perhaps he 'admired' their striker (purely for his footballing prowess, of course). And if you want to maintain your credibility within the footballing community you must also lie like this. The reasons you're meant to give for supporting a team are as follows:

- You were born near their ground
- They're your local team
- A close (preferably dead) member of your family supported them for years
- Your dad always supported their rivals and you want to piss him off.

So, if anyone asks, you support Arsenal because your: 'dead dad used to watch them week in week out for years' and not because: 'that Thierry Henry had such a sexy accent in those car ads. I'd like to show him what va-va-voom means.'

spread yourself

If you've already committed yourself to an ugly bunch of non-league hoofers, you can, however, legitimately lend your support to a handful of other clubs under the 'armchair' classification of fandom. You mustn't feel guilty, it's not cheating; think of it as if you're entering into a mutually agreeable open relationship – you have needs that one team just can't satisfy. And as long as you don't 'hop into bed' with a team that's in the same league as the one you support, then no one will get hurt.

Most fans have at least three other teams who they'll 'keep an eye out for' and they'll quite freely admit to having flimsy reasons for following them (nice shirts, that sort of thing). To fully appreciate your status as an armchair fan, you'll want to have a team from each domestic league in your portfolio, together with a foreign club. And of course, it goes without saying that you'll also root for your national squad when international competitions come around.

Bafflingly, true footie nuts will extend their portfolio still further with dozens of teams that they watch out for just because those teams' performances just might affect the league positions of their primary and armchair clubs. This is why your man will happily sit and watch a match featuring two seemingly obscure teams and shout at the screen with the same passion as if he's at the FA Cup Final.

the clubs

Still can't make your mind up who to pledge your allegiance to? Here's our guide to ten of the biggest clubs in the country, each with a natty piece of man-impressing trivia...

ARSENAL

home ground

Highbury

in a nutshell

They used to be branded 'boring boring Arsenal' due to their uninspiring style of play, but things have changed recently and the 'Gunners' are perhaps now one of the most exciting teams to watch in Britain. And one of the best in Europe.

finest hour

The 2001–02 season saw the team clinch their third 'Double'. They beat arch rivals Chelsea to win the FA Cup, and then went on to win the Premiership at Manchester United's home ground, Old Trafford.

pulling trivia

The Londoners play in red and white because a posse of Nottingham Forest players joined the squad in 1895 and brought their old kit along with them. The then cash-strapped club figured it would be cheaper to dress the rest of the team in the same colours rather than buy a new kit for everyone.

MANCHESTER UNITED

home ground

Old Trafford

in a nutshell

The best supported (yet most hated) club in the world dominated British football in the 1990s but they've won relatively little in recent years – but that's not to say that they're no good anymore, they're still capable of brilliant football.

finest hour

In 1999, Man U won the FA Cup, the Premiership and the Champions League – the elusive 'Treble'. Later that year, Sir Alex

Ferguson's men went on to become World Club Champions in the Inter Continental Cup.

pulling trivia

The 'Red Devils' were first formed in 1878 by a group of workers in a railway yard. Hence the club's original name: Newton Heath Lancashire and Yorkshire Railway.

CHELSEA

home ground

Stamford Bridge

in a nutshell

The pundits always begin the season by speculating 'Could this be Chelsea's year?' and in 2004, it finally was – even if it did take them half a century to do it. The Blues' mercurial manager, José Mourinho (AKA: the George Clooney of the Premiership) spurred them onto win the Premiership and they had a damn good stab at the Champions League, too. The club's currently leading yet another renaissance in British Football.

finest hour

1998 was a pretty good year for the Blues. They won the European Cup Winners' Cup, the Coca Cola Cup and the European Super Cup – whatever that is.

pulling trivia

Chelsea's playing record at Manchester United's traditionally intimidating home ground is astounding. They have only lost a handful of times at Old Trafford in 37 years, with a record of 11 wins, 14 draws and 4 defeats.

RANGERS

home ground

Ibrox, Glasgow

in a nutshell

The Scottish Premier League is usually a two-horse race, with Celtic and Rangers (the so-called 'Old Firm') battling it out for glory. Rangers have been coming a close second recently, but it'll be their turn to lift some cups soon. Not any European ones though, they're rubbish away from Scottish soil.

finest hour

In 1989 the club began a Scottish League Championship-winning run that saw them lift the trophy nine times in succession.

pulling trivia

Alex McLeish is only the tenth Rangers manager in the 124-year history of the club. Before William Wilton was given the title of 'manager' in 1899, a committee picked the team.

CELTIC

home ground

Celtic Park, Glasgow

in a nutshell

Celtic are blessed with a masterful manager (Martin O'Neil, who is routinely linked with every coach's job that ever becomes vacant), the biggest crowds in Britain and some phenomenally talented players. Which is why they win. A lot.

finest hour

The 1966–1967 season was rather nifty. They won the League, the League Cup and – a first for any British team – the European Cup.

pulling trivia

Bizarrely, when Celtic played in Bucharest in 1972, the fans at a hotel in the city were entertained by Elizabeth Taylor and Richard Burton who threw a post-match champagne and caviar party.

LIVERPOOL

home ground

Anfield

in a nutshell

Liverpool were HUGELY successful in the 1980s, but they've underachieved for over a decade – the turning point seemingly being the 1989 Hillsborough tragedy when 96 supporters died. 'Reds' will be quick to point out that they won the treble in 2001, but it wasn't *the* Treble – two of the cups they won are as coveted as Tupperware beakers.

finest hour

They've won a warehouse full of trophies over the years, but the greatest night in Liverpool's history remains when they lifted the European Cup for the first time in 1977.

pulling trivia

Liverpool fans began the trend for wearing designer labels to football matches. They began 'acquiring' trendy clothes while playing in Europe in the 1970s and 1980s.

TOTTENHAM HOTSPUR

home ground

White Hart Lane, London

in a nutshell

Historically, Spurs were one of English football's 'big six' clubs, but today they struggle to make it into the top half of the Premier League and seem to be forever in the papers with one off-the-pitch crisis after another. Arch rivals of Arsenal.

finest hour

Two Argentine international players, Ricardo Villa and Ossie

Ardiles, Inspired Spurs to win two FA Cup titles on the trot in 1981 and 1982.

pulling trivia

The club took its name from Harry Hotspur, a character in the Shakespearean play *Henry IV, Part 1.*

EVERTON

home ground

Goodison Park

in a nutshell

Though they're unpredictable nowadays, Everton's history is laced with triumph. Only Liverpool, Manchester United and Arsenal have won more league titles than them and their haul of five FA Cups is also among the best in the country.

finest hour

1985 must've been sweet for the 'Toffees': they won the league; got through to the FA Cup final; won the FA Charity Shield; and lifted the European Cup Winners' Cup.

pulling trivia

The most goals scored for one club was 349 by Everton's Dixie Dean. He still holds the record for the most league goals in a season with 60 in 39 matches (1927–28).

NEWCASTLE UNITED

home ground

St James' Park

in a nutshell

For a team that have won relatively little in their 125 years, Newcastle United are forever in the public eye – you can put that down to a fervent set of fans (the Toon Army) and some high profile signings (Keegan, Shearer, etc) over the years.

finest hour

The Magpies last won the league back in 1927 and most recently picked up the FA Cup in 1955. To say that the Toon Army is desperate for glory is an understatement.

pulling trivia

In 1987 Newcastle became the first British club to sign a Brazilian player. Unfortunately, Francisco Ernami Lima de Silva – better known as Mirandinha – was useless and flew back to his homeland within two years.

LEEDS UNITED

home ground

Elland Road

in a nutshell

The hapless 'Whites' are now known for making monstrous mistakes. They sold Eric Cantona to Manchester United (he went on to become one of football's most influential players ever), tried (and failed) to buy success in Europe, and suffered financial collapse in 2004. Then they got relegated.

finest hour

Under manager Don Revie, Leeds won armfuls of trophies. Most notably: two league championships (1968–69, 1973–74), the League Cup in 1968, and the FA Cup in 1972.

pulling trivia

Leeds are responsible for one of the biggest British European Cup wins of all time. In 1969–70, they beat SFK Lyn of Norway by a huge 10–0 (and then went on to win the second leg 6–0).

who does what

Of the 11 players that make up a side, goalkeepers seemingly have the only easily recognisable role: they must taunt the opposition fans when the ref's not looking, shout at their team mates and occasionally leap around in front of the goalmouth like a Presidential bodyguard taking a bullet. But what do the rest of the team do? And for that matter, how do the so-called back-room staff earn a living?

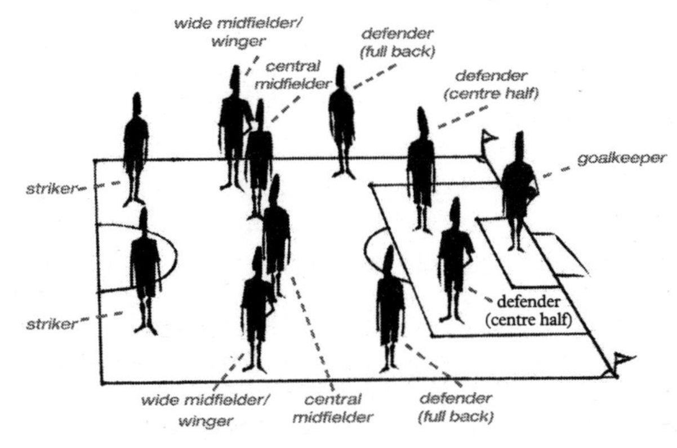

striker *(e.g. Wayne Rooney)*

Scores goals. That's it. Unfortunately, they don't tend to be very bright so strikers hardly ever come back and defend – there's every chance they'll hoof the ball into their own goal.

full back *(e.g. Ashley Cole)*

Full-backs are defenders and can play on either side of the pitch (wide) or provide support for the midfielders. Modern full backs push forward and supply balls to the striker.

central midfielder *(e.g. David Beckham)*

Central midfielders are crucial to the success of a team. They run around like dogs with their tails on fire in the middle of the pitch, tackling the opposition, passing the ball to the striker or even having a bash at goal themselves.

wide midfielder/winger *(e.g. Ryan Giggs)*

These are the men to watch: they sprint up the sides of the pitch and, if they're any good, outsmart the defenders with some fancy footwork. They then kick the ball into the middle for the striker to tap into the goal. That's the idea, anyway.

sweeper

This is a very specialised role which is favoured on the Continent. A sweeper will play behind the defence and in front of the goalkeeper, and provide backup for the defenders. He'll take on anyone, basically.

manager

The manager is the person in charge of the team. They'll choose tactics, sign new players, pick the team on match day and tell them what to do on the pitch. He won't usually organise the day-to-day running of the club as a business; that's the Chief Executive's job.

coach

Large vehicle that takes players to matches.

coach (2)

A coach differs from a manager in that he is more concerned with the training, dietary requirements and fitness of the team.

director of football

Directors of Football tend to be respected former players brought in to offer their expert opinion (when things are going wrong but the club can't sack the manager for legal reasons, usually). They'll work closely with the manager and suggest tactics for upcoming games.

2

Don't know your Vase from your Euro?

a guide to leagues, cups and competitions

You wouldn't know it from the amount of time they seem to spend drinking lager, fighting outside nightclubs and engaging in group sex, but football players actually play the game quite often. The season begins in August and ends the following May and in theory a team can be entered into four comps at the same time, which makes for a lot of fixtures. Add training sessions into the schedule and that leaves virtually no time for the poor loves to count their cash or cultivate ridiculous haircuts.

world cup

worth cancelling a shopping trip for?

Yes. More so than any other competition.

The fact that they come around only once every four years makes them special. The fact that they unite the nation to such an extent that even your grandma can be provoked to swear at a televised football match makes them special. The fact that the Office Footie Nut shaves a St George's Cross onto his head or gets a tattoo of a dragon on his bum makes them, er, interesting. The next time the World Cup's staged, get signed off sick for the whole of the competition and watch every single match just for the quality of the football. If you're not smitten by the game already, it'll be like embarking on an intense life-long love affair. But without the sex, obviously.

european championships

worth cancelling a shopping trip for?

Absolutely.

You must remember Euro 1996, when the whole country went football loopy. The sun shone; Chris Evans encouraged his breakfast show listeners to pull sickies and watch matches in the pub instead; Frank Skinner and David Baddiel caught the public's imagination with *Three Lions*; and the England team *truly* could have won it. Greece – traditionally rubbish at football – caused an upset by winning the last championships (Portugal 2004) and they'll be back to defend their title four years down the line in Austria and Switzerland. There are qualifying rounds held prior to the event itself (the 'Finals'), and it's during these matches that the tiny nations such as Luxembourg and Malta get knocked out.

Just 16 teams take part in the Finals and because of the way the fixtures are structured, it is possible to get through to the final itself by winning just three matches. Don't point this out if one of our national squads ever makes it through though, as it's something that fans prefer to ignore.

premiership

worth cancelling a shopping trip for?

Definitely.

Sometimes known as the Premier League (it also changes its sponsor from time to time – it's Barclays at the mo), this is the most important league in England. Every year, 20 teams battle it out to be the best in the land by notching up three points for every win and one for a draw. The club with the most points come the end of the season (May) is then presented with a lovely sparkly cup. Saying that, just three teams presently have a realistic chance of actually winning it at the moment (Manchester United, Chelsea and Arsenal), the rest mill about in the middle of the table hoping to finish at least fourth – if they do so, they automatically qualify to play in one of the lucrative European competitions the following season. The bottom three teams are relegated.

football league

worth cancelling a shopping trip for?

Yep – even a Saturday shoe-shop.

The rest of the football league may not be as glitzy as the Premiership, but it still throws up some excellent entertainment. Well, perhaps not in the lowest division, some of those teams are RUBBISH. The league is split into three divisions, but they're not called division one, two and three. Oh no.

There's The Championship, League One and League Two and they're all structured in the same way as the Premiership (three points for a win and all that). The idea is to get the most points, obviously, but the runners up also get automatically promoted to the league above. As do the winners of the play offs (see below)...

scottish premier league

Worth cancelling a shopping trip for?

Depends who's playing.

Unfortunately, the quality of the football in the SPL isn't quite the same as it is south of the border. To be honest, for the most part it's downright dull and watching the teams from lower in the league play can be like having a flashback to the fat dads of the 1970s. The two richest teams in Scotland – Rangers and Celtic – dominate the league, and one of them always seems to run away with the title weeks before the end of the season, which can get a bit boring. The real competition seems to be for third and fourth place nowadays.

league play-offs

worth cancelling a shopping trip for?

Oh yes.

The winners and runners up of all the leagues can be decided weeks before the end of the season if they amass enough points. However, three or more teams can be promoted and these other teams are decided by an end-of-the-season play off competition. The clubs in third, fourth, fifth, sixth and seventh position play against each other and the two top teams from these matches then go forward to a swanky final to decide the ultimate winner. It's a little unfair for the team that originally finished third, but it provides some thrilling football. Each team is desperate to be promoted y'see (they'll get paid more in a higher league) and they battle it out as if they're playing for the last virgin in the stands.

FA cup

worth cancelling a shopping trip for?

God yes.

The Football Association (FA) first proposed the idea of a 'challenge cup' in 1871 and it has gone on to become one of the country's great sporting institutions. In fact, fans from all over the world keep an eye out for it. Why? Well, because of the so-called 'romance' – the fact that literally any club can win it, from those at the top of the Premiership to lowly teams made up of part-time postmen and the like. The top clubs usually triumph of course, but there is still fair bit of 'giant killing' to be enjoyed; usually at the hands of teams like Southport and Yeovil Town. It's a knockout competition and teams play each other only once, so as soon as they lose, they're out of the running. The final's held every May, but, curiously, if it's a draw after extra time, everyone has to go home and they play it again a few days later.

FA charity shield

worth cancelling a shopping trip for?

Nah.

The Charity Shield is the traditional curtain-raiser to the English domestic football campaign, when the winners of the previous season's Premiership and FA Cup play each other for the first piece of silverware: a big plate that no one cares about winning. No one except for the eventual winners of course, and they'll then brag about it for weeks.

league cup

worth cancelling a shopping trip for?

Depends who's playing.

On 'paper' the yearly League Cup (or the Carling Cup as it's currently known) should be as coveted as the FA Cup; the fixtures are drawn by lottery so lowly teams can take on the biggest in the league and it's a knockout format again, but it doesn't quite have the aforementioned 'romance' that the other cup's got. If your team gets through to the final it's definitely worth a trip to the Millennium Stadium to cheer them on though.

intertoto cup

worth cancelling a shopping trip for?

Nope.

UEFA, the big cheeses of European football, have this to say about this bizarrely-named annual competition: 'The UEFA Intertoto Cup is a summer competition which allows clubs which do not qualify for the UEFA Champions League or UEFA Cup to sample the unique atmosphere of European club football – with the three eventual 'winners' actually going on to take part in the UEFA Cup.' Sounds rubbish, doesn't it? It is.

FA trophy

worth cancelling a shopping trip for?

Not even a trip to ASDA.

The Football Association dreamed up the FA Trophy in 1969, a yearly knockout competition for non-league clubs with the incentive of an appearance at Wembley (or Villa Park recently) for the finalists. The final will usually attract a huge crowd, but it will be generally ignored by the mainstream media.

FA vase

worth cancelling a shopping trip for?

Nah.

The Vase used to be known as the Amateur Cup and it's still basically a competition for non-professional teams. In 1999, 446 clubs entered and to win it is quite an achievement, but the competition is generally ignored by those not directly affected.

olympics

worth cancelling a shopping trip for?

Hell no.

Despite the fact that football was introduced to the Games over 100 years ago, this is such a non-event that England don't even bother sending a team (there's a bit of politics involved too because we'd all have to muck in and form a Great Britain team which no one wants to do) and the 2004 final was held in a half-empty stadium. Interestingly though, women's football was first played at the 1996 Olympic Games, where the final attracted a world record crowd for a women's sporting event of 76,000 people. Result.

confederations cup

worth cancelling a shopping trip for?

Good god, no.

Just forget you even heard of it.

3

Enough with the offside salt cellar analogy!

the rules made easy

You're out shoe shopping and – hang on a minute! – you notice that a sales assistant is marking down what looks like a fab pair of Manolo Blahniks in your size that would go perfectly with that dress you've got your eye on next door. The trouble is, another girl has spotted the reduced shoes too and she's between you and the till. To make matters worse, your mate's got your purse and she's busy at the back of the store considering whether she can get away with trying on a pair of shoes without putting on the store's manky old pop socks. The rules of shopping dictate that you can't barge past your opponent, grab the shoes and wait at the front of the queue until your friend throws you some money – that would earn you a retail red card. What you have to do is get your friend to throw you the purse first, *then* you can barge past the other girl, grab the shoes and clinch the deal.

If you can understand that, you can understand the dreaded offside rule.

It's a 'dreaded' rule because, as a fan in training, you will be asked by men to explain it even more times than you'll be asked which team you support. And if you get it wrong, they will then sneer and take great delight in teaching it to you. Badly. With bits of crockery, usually.

The rule was instituted to stop strikers spending the whole game next to the opposition's goalkeeper waiting for one of their mates to hoof the ball up to them so that they could score. What the football authorities did was to bring in a rule that meant that the striker had to move back up the pitch when the opposition's defenders did. In a nutshell, it goes like this: a player (that's you, out shoe shopping) is in an offside position if they are nearer to the opposition's goal mouth (the till) than both the ball (your purse), the goalkeeper and any of their other players (the other shopper).

However, that player is not offside if all this is going on in his own half, or if someone passes the ball to him from a throw in, a goal kick, or a corner. There are a few other variations to complicate things, but you really don't need to know

about them. No one will mock you for pointing out an offside that turns out not to be on some technicality, they'll love you all the more for it in fact. Men are funny like that.

You probably learned back in primary school that boys like to tell tales on each other. They'd probably say things like: 'Umm... Miss, Johnny's eaten my lunch,' or 'I just saw Pete wee into his own mouth,' and unfortunately this unhealthy trait remains strong well into their old age. Not the weeing into the mouth trait, men usually grow out of that before puberty, it's the pointing out wrongdoings thing that they can't shake off. Take a chap watching a match for example, he'll spend at least a third of the game screaming at the referee – even if he's just on the telly, bizarrely – pointing out fouls, handballs and all manner of indiscretions. And then he'll bring the whole sorry lot to the attention of his mates the next time he's in the pub. Sadly, to pass yourself off as a genuine fan and not someone who merely likes watching powerfully-built men running around in shorts, you'll have to familiarise yourself with the reasons why 'that was never a penalty' and a few other minor rules...

the basics

Now try and prevent yourself from yawning, but the game begins with 11 players per side and all must be in their own half when the referee blows his whistle to kick off. A manager can replace up to three of his players with substitutes (meaning players that are known as substitutes – not other things like goats or chairs or calculators, that's just crazy) during the match, though if it's a friendly match (i.e. one that doesn't count towards any cup or competition) he can replace six players if he fancies, and give everyone a bit of exercise.

The rules state that the first touch of the ball must go forward from the centre-spot and the game is restarted after a goal and also at the start of the second half in exactly the same way. Talking of halves, there are two of them, obviously, and each lasts for 45 minutes. The players have 15 minutes break at half time, during which they can either reapply their hair products and have a relaxing massage or get shouted at by the manager – usually it's the latter.

Additional time is allowed at the end of each half by the referee to make up for time lost through substitutions and the treatment of injured players. Most of this extra time will be added on at the end of the second half, and predicting how much time will be given is a futile task; some referees can choose to add on four minutes just because some naked lummox ran around the pitch for 30 seconds. (Although, if it's your team that's losing, it might be wise to become that lummox and buy your boys some time.)

the confusing part

If it's the finishing stages of a cup competition, extra-time is often played if the score is still level, and this is where it can get hard to understand. The teams will stay on the pitch, have a little breather, a slurp of energy drink, and then they'll play one of the following:

- Two full fifteen-minute periods
- A maximum of two fifteen-minute periods, but it's all over as soon as one team scores (this is known as a 'golden goal')

- A maximum of two fifteen-minute periods, but if one team's ahead after fifteen minutes that team is declared the winner (a 'silver goal'). If not, they play the next fifteen minutes.

If the result remains deadlocked at the end of all these shenanigans, a penalty shootout determines the victors. In its simplest terms, each team has five pot shots at goal and the team with the most goals at the end wins. In the heat of the moment though, it can get incredibly baffling and sometimes even the teams involved don't know if they're up or down. If a shootout ever occurs when you're watching and you're in doubt, ask someone to explain it. If you can pick a chap that's young, gorgeous and seemingly single, that's all to the better.

officials

The man in black with the whistle is obviously the referee and it's him who takes charge of a match, along with his two 'bitches' – though they prefer to be known as assistant referees (they're the ones who run up and down the side of the pitch and used to be called linesmen). The assistant refs help out with decisions such as throw ins and offsides and will sometimes have a better view of incidents such as fouls.

The ref, however, is The Man. He enforces the laws of the game, awards free kicks if there is any foul play and keeps a check on the time. The ref can also postpone, stop, suspend or cancel a match if there are weather or crowd problems. He can also give the players a stern telling off if they've got their socks rolled down – international rules state that they have to completely cover the shin pads.

There's also a fourth official – the nattily named fourth official – who spends his time on the touchline, where the teams sit. He makes sure the managers don't run onto the pitch ranting and raving, helps out with substitutions and holds up an electronic board that tells everyone how much extra time is going to be played.

why's he blowing that thing *again*? – a quick guide

throw in

Given the amount of skill they're supposed to have, you'd have thought that professional players would at least manage to keep the ball within the confines of the pitch but no, they're forever booting it into the stands. When the ball fully crosses the touchlines (the longest sides of the pitch), it's thrown back into play by a player from whichever team didn't touch it last. You might have to re-read that last sentence, but it makes sense, honestly.

goal kick

When a member of the attacking team last touches the ball before it goes over either of the lines at the ends of the pitch, the defending team get to begin play again. The keeper usually takes care of this, and he does so by placing the ball anywhere within the goal area (the small box in front of the goal) and, usually, hoofing it impressively hard and high. Everyone else has to stay out of the penalty area (the bigger box that contains the smaller box) while he does this.

corner kick

The corner kick – it's usually just known as a corner though – is a method of restarting play when a member of the defending team last touches the ball before it goes over either of the lines at the ends of the pitch. Goals are often scored from corners, so defending teams do all they can to prevent them from happening. If there's no other option, they often purposely kick the ball out to the side for a throw in instead.

direct free kick

A direct free kick is what happens when play stops, a wall of players holding their family jewels stands between the ball and the goal, and a member of the attacking team wallops the ball at goal as hard as he can. A referee will award a direct free kick if a player hits, kicks, charges at, spits at, trips, holds, jumps at or pushes an opponent, or commits a hand-ball. 'Severe' fouls, basically.

It's worth pointing out that handball is only given when a

player touches a ball with his hand or arm on purpose – in other words if he hits the ball, not if the ball hits him. Refs are usually pretty hot on this, well, except if the player is a certain Diego Maradona and it happens during a crucial World Cup match, in which case they'll turn a blind eye.

indirect free kick

An indirect free kick differs from the direct version in that the ball has to be passed to another player before a shot on goal can be made. They're handed out for the lesser crimes of impeding a player's progress, playing in a dangerous manner, preventing a goalkeeper from releasing the ball from his hands or throwing snowballs at gentlemen in top hats.* An indirect free kick can also be awarded against the keeper if he goofs – though this rarely happens.

penalty

See all those reasons above for awarding a direct free kick? They're the same ones for giving a penalty – it's just that the offence has occurred inside the guilty player's own penalty area.

red card, yellow card

A yellow card is like a final written warning at work; screw up again and you're out. There are seven different offences that can earn you a yellow from the ref, they're all far too boring to bother with ('dissent by word or action, entering or re-entering the pitch without the referee's permission,' etc.),

*That last bit was made up.

but they all boil down to the same thing: mucking about a bit too much.

Players are shown a red card and sent off if they receive two yellow cards in one match, or if they commit one of six reeeaaally naughty offences:

- Serious foul play (knowingly doing something that could seriously injure another player)
- Violent conduct such as throwing a punch
- Spitting at an opponent or another person
- A player other than the goalkeeper denies an 'obvious goalscoring opportunity' by touching the ball with his hands
- A goalkeeper intentionally handles the ball outside his goal area.

4

The good, the bad, and the Beardsley... players to watch out for

Poor Peter Beardsley. The now-retired Newcastle midfielder scored over 250 goals in his career, was described by Keggy Keegle (Kevin Keegan) as 'Simply the best, better than all the rest' and played for his country 59 times, which is a lot. Yet mention his name in any pub in the country and his 'unconventional' features will be mentioned before anything else. He was ugly, mind.

In any other sphere of life, ridiculing another person's physical appearance would be quite rightly frowned upon, but curiously it's a vital and socially accepted ingredient of football culture. In honour of this glorious bastion of political incorrectness (and because some matches can be dead boring to watch), the following fantasy team features a handful of the ugliest footballers you can see playing today, together with some of the best players to watch out for, and a selection of bad boys. Because everyone likes a bit of rough from time to time...

goalkeeper

Ugly

BRAD FRIEDEL

current club
Blackburn

shirt number
1

phwoar factor
Barely registers on the scale.

On the plus side, the 34-year-old keeper is a 6'3' bear of a man with VERY BIG HANDS, but that balding pate and his upturned hog-nose are hard to overlook. And, it's a sweeping generalisation, but being American and a sportsman, you can bet he wears white socks with sandals. Eughh. That said, he's a fair old player, having established himself as Blackburn's number one keeper and has shown the kind of form that attracted the likes of Galtasaray (hugely successful Turkish club) and Liverpool a few years back (indeed, many Reds still question why the club ever let him go). The former ginger has over 80 international caps to his name and has represented his country at the Olympics and the World Cup.

defenders

Good

JOHN TERRY

current club
Chelsea

shirt number
26

phwoar factor
Horny body, nice hair, bit dim.

Since winning the Chelsea Young Player of the Year award in 1998–99, the Blues' young captain has become a Premiership footballing superstar. He won the big boys' version of the gong two years later, but the sudden adulation seemed to turn his head a bit and shortly afterwards he was arrested following an 'incident' outside a nightclub. The 2002–03 season was therefore make-or-break for one of the country's best young players, and, fortunately, he rose to the challenge. He even scored six goals for Chelsea, which is a big deal for a defender. Even more impressively, during the following season he was one of the only players who avoided Claudio Ranieri's (his then boss, AKA: The Tinkerman) er, tinkering, by playing in pretty much every match of the season. Terry now applies his striker-stopping skills to the England defence. He's also hotly tipped to take over his country's captaincy from David Beckham.

Ugly

ANDY O'BRIEN

current club
Newcastle United

shirt number
5

phwoar factor
Oh dear.

When Bradford's 'Mr Reliable' signed to Newcastle in 2001, he wasn't met with the usual Toon Army enthusiasm: 'I probably wasn't the most exciting signing in the world from a Newcastle fan's point of view,' he lamented. And how the Geordie girls' hearts must have sank when they set eyes on a man who can only be described as the inspiration for the Mr Men's pointy-faced Mr Rush. As a defender though, he's pretty tasty and he even turned down a chance to play for England, opting to pursue his international career with the Republic of Ireland instead.

GARY NEVILLE

current club
Manchester United

shirt number
2

phwoar factor
After a dozen Bacardi Breezers, you might just be tempted.

Having joined Manchester United on 'schoolboy forms' in 1991, Neville is a lynchpin of the all-conquering club and has picked up six league winners' medals along with a satchel-full of other awards. Interestingly, he plays at the club alongside his brother, Phil, who also joins him in the England squad. A solid, dependable player with a vast wealth of experience and tactical knowledge, the fans love him because he's a United fan to his boots. He can't grow a decent moustache though.

Good

WAYNE BRIDGE

current club
Chelsea

shirt number
18

phwoar factor
Good strong jaw and powerfully built. Grrr.

Another Chelsea player who's among Britain's best, Wayne is a naturally left-sided defender who likes to run about all over the pitch like a streaker being chased by the police and he delivers deadly crosses whenever he gets the chance. The reason behind this is probably because he started his career in midfield and he still wants to be up where the goal action is. A rapid ascent with England saw him coming on twice as a sub at the 2002 World Cup and he's slowly consolidating his position as a first choice player. Bridge doesn't seem to know what he's doing with his hair though, which is always a shame.

midfielders

LEE BOWYER

current club
Newcastle United

shirt number
29

phwoar factor
Frightening. Just frightening.

While Bowyer's unsightly mug keeps him out of the glossies, his bad boy antics mean that he's seldom far from the front pages of the papers. He was arrested and subsequently fined for a rampage in a McDonalds in 1996, was charged by the FA for 'foul and abusive language towards a match official' during a Gunners clash in 2001 (a tactic that he repeated the following year), whacked Liverpool's Gary McAllister in 2002, and that's not to mention the infamous court case when he was at Leeds (of which he was later cleared). Or the alleged melée in a lap-dancing club in 2000. Or the extended bans for dope in 1995 and stamping on the head of a downed Malaga player in 2002. Cripes!

Bad

DENNIS WISE

current club
Millwall

shirt number
19

phwoar factor
Blessed with eyes made for mischief.

Don't be fooled by his cheeky-chappie appearance, the Millwall player/manager is well known for being, er, tempestuous. Wise – who once said, 'If I had to use one word to describe myself, it would be fighter' – started scrapping as a nipper and by the age of 18 had been found guilty of a road rage incident. A drink-driving conviction followed and then, in 1994, came 'The Menace's' defining moment of madness. Having been on a night out with his mates, he hailed a cab, but went loopy when the driver refused to take him where he wanted to go. He smashed his fist through the glass partition and caught hold of the driver's throat, before the police turned up. Textbook Wise, that.

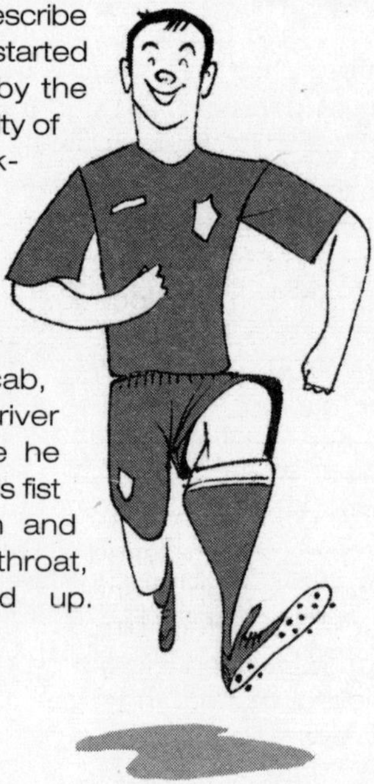

Bad

ROY KEANE

current club
Manchester United

shirt number
16

phwoar factor
A guilty pleasure.

Usually pictured eyes wide and with his veins looking to explode, Keane's presence livens up Sunday's back pages, whether he's crunching his fellow professionals or berating his club's own supporters for supposedly enjoying prawn sandwiches in the corporate boxes more than the football. In 1993 he was thrown out of a wine bar after ignoring warnings to behave himself, and a year later he was banned from a Manchester club for spitting and swearing. In 1997 he was barred from his local pub after a series of bust-ups, but stopped drinking shortly after spending a night in a Manchester police station. But while he recognises his mistakes, Keano's not about to apologise for his actions. When asked if he regretted a horrific foul on Alf-Inge Haaland, Keane replied: '. . . fuck him. What goes around comes around. He got his just rewards. He fucked me over and my attitude is an eye for an eye.'

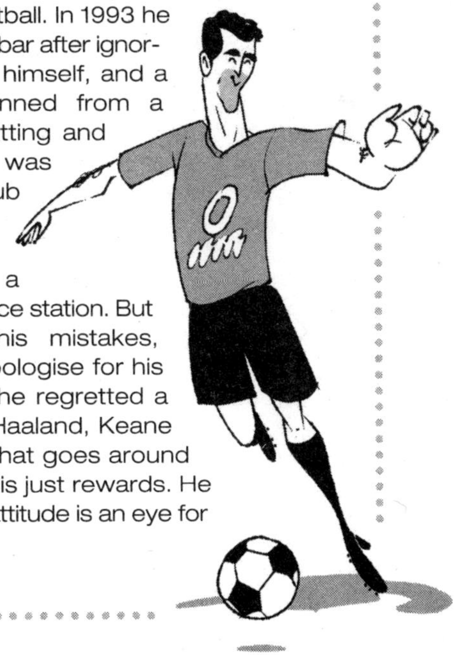

Good

ROBERT PIRES

current club
Arsenal

shirt number
7

phwoar factor
So French. So gorgeous.

Often dubbed a 'French midfield maestro' by the papers, Pires was part of the all-conquering French national team of World Cup 1998 and Euro 2000, setting up the Golden Goal which secured France the title of European champions. And he comes up with the goods at Arsenal too, handing the strikers goals on plates and gobbling up as many as he can for himself. He managed 19 goals in 2003–04, helping the Gunners to glory with another league championship, though he couldn't work his magic for France again, and had a very disappointing Euro 2004. However, catching a glimpse of his bod when he's swapping shirts with the opposition can make up for any disappointment.

strikers

WAYNE ROONEY

current club
Manchester United

shirt number
8

phwoar factor
Purleease! Well, perhaps if he paid you.

Admittedly, he looks like he could understudy for Shrek, but there's every possibility that young Rooney could turn into an international footballing legend. At 16 he made his top flight debut against Spurs (for Everton) and holds the records for England's youngest cap and youngest ever scorer. Manchester United snapped him up for a huge fee after he wowed the crowds at Euro 2004, but it's perhaps too early to tell if he's going to be 'The One'. Hopefully, Sir Alex Ferguson (Manchester United's manager) will guide him and nurture his natural talent – and prevent all this adulation going to his head. What is certain, however, is that Rooney has awesome talent, the strength and fearlessness of a boxer and, crucially, unwavering confidence.

Good

THIERRY HENRY

current club
Arsenal

shirt number
14

phwoar factor
The ultimate: athletic, charming and intelligent.

Unlike Rooney, Henry is a confirmed legend who is considered by many to be the most exciting player to watch in the world. The Arsenal striker made history by becoming the first player to win the Football Writers' Association's prestigious Footballer of the Year award two years running, and his list of honours is frankly embarrassing: World Cup winner (1998), European Championship winner (2000), FA Cup winner (2002, 2003), Premier League winner (2002, 2004), etc. He's a winner, basically. Among other things, Henry is well known for his exceptional pace and neat finishing which puts him at, or near, the top of the Premiership top scorers list each season. As Newcastle manager Graham Souness explains: 'the only way to stop him is with an AK 47.'

5

Say what?!

the unfathomable world of footie-speak

Commentators, footballers, managers and spectators all talk about the game in roughly the same language: a mad, seemingly impenetrable language of clichés and nonsensical drivel. However, to fully appreciate the game you'll need to get to grips with at least some key phrases. You'll probably never use them in your everyday speech, but at least you'll be clued up come the next big match...

In what was probably a first for the sport, a footie manager actually admitted in

2002 that he had run out of new things to say when he was interviewed by the media. A despondent Billy Stark, whose team St Johnstone had just been beaten 1–0 by Aberdeen, said to a group of hacks at the post-match press conference: 'I have spent the last 15 minutes thinking of something different to say but it's pretty much the same script – it's like a long-playing record.' Sadly, Billy couldn't quite help himself and promptly launched into a barrage of hackneyed clichés including: 'I was quite positive going into half time but that goal lifted Aberdeen and deflated us' and: 'There was nothing in the game. We looked pretty comfortable defensively,' but the thought was there.

Footie speak can seem like an impenetrable tongue, but it's based around the same phrases and clichés repeated week in, week out – although each section of the footballing community has a different dialect, if you will. For example, if a team's losing, a fan in the pub might say: 'I reckon they're gonna get beat here.' This, you'll appreciate, is perfectly understandable to the entry-level fan (despite it being grammatically incorrect), but a manager being interviewed at half time would instead say something like: 'We've got our backs against the wall'. Whereas a TV commentator might say: 'They're staring down the barrel of defeat,' which is just crazy talk.

The worst offender used to be a chap called Ron Atkinson who used to commentate for ITV until... well, until his big mouth got the better of him and he got sacked for making a racist comment on air. The former Manchester United manager had clearly been in the game for too long and at the end of his career used to spout all sorts of nonsense that used to leave viewers and his co-commentators speechless. For example, a goal scored at the end of a match by a team already in the lead was routinely described as 'a little bit of afters' while another of his favourites – 'he's given it a little bit of the eyebrows' – defies translation. However, thanks to unimaginative reporting, fine examples of Big Ron's English (Ronglish) can still be heard on every TV and radio station in the land.

Interestingly, just one commentator from the scores of football programmes on British radio, terrestrial TV and satellite TV does things differently. And that's Stuart Hall. You may remember him from *It's A Knockout* in the 1970s and 80s – he was the one that laughed like an idiot when the contestants fell over their comedy boots and spilled coloured water over themselves. Hall's poetic prose can be heard each week on BBC Radio Five Live, normally at a Manchester City or Everton game, and presumably after an extended pre-match lunch. Which is probably why he comes out with quotes like this: 'And here we are at the coliseum, with a match of titanic proportions about to take place. Will the gladiatorial figurine of Owen add to his mighty goals tally?' Bonkers, but entertaining to listen to.

It's worth noting that foreign commentators have a different take on things too. They're not bound by the British code of impartiality, shun catchphrases in general (they seem to like 'gooooooooooooaaaaaaaaaallllllllll', though), and just scream for whichever team they fancy. A perfect example of this is courtesy of a Norwegian broadcaster called Bjørge Lillelien who, after Norway shockingly defeated England 2–1 at Wembley in 1981, screamed in English into his microphone: 'Lord Nelson! Lord Beaverbrook! Sir Winston Churchill! Sir Anthony Eden! Clement Attlee! Henry Cooper! Lady Diana! Maggie Thatcher – can you hear me, Maggie Thatcher? Your boys took one hell of a beating! Your boys took one hell of a beating!' Nuts, plain nuts, but perhaps the best piece of sports commentary ever (come out with it whenever anyone trumpets the 'They think it's all over speech' as the best piece of sports commentary ever and then marvel as they suddenly begin nodding sagely).

But while commentators come up with all manner of oral caca, at least they're just trying to be entertaining. Footballers and their managers generally talk shite in front of microphones and think they sound like they're discussing international policy down at the Foreign Office – just listen to Manchester United manager Sir Alex Ferguson, who once said: 'When an Italian says it's pasta I check under the sauce to make sure. They are innovators of the smokescreen.'

However, of all those who talk publicly about the game, there is none more accomplished at talking utter incomprehensible rot than Kevin Keegan; and being a pundit, a former player, a true fan and a former manager, he fulfils all the criteria. Quite how he was appointed England boss after making gaffes like these is almost incomprehensible...

the wisdom of keggy*

'He can't speak Turkey, but you can tell he's delighted.'

'I came to Nantes two years ago and it's much the same today, except that it's totally different.'

'I know what is around the corner – I just don't know where the corner is. But the onus is on us to perform and we must control the bandwagon.'

'I'd love to be a mole on the wall in the Liverpool dressing room at half-time.'

'Young Gareth Barry – he's young'

'They're the second best team in the world, and there's no higher praise than that.'

'They don't come every three days, like they come after this one.'

'There's a slight doubt about only one player, and that's Tony Adams, who definitely won't be playing tomorrow.'

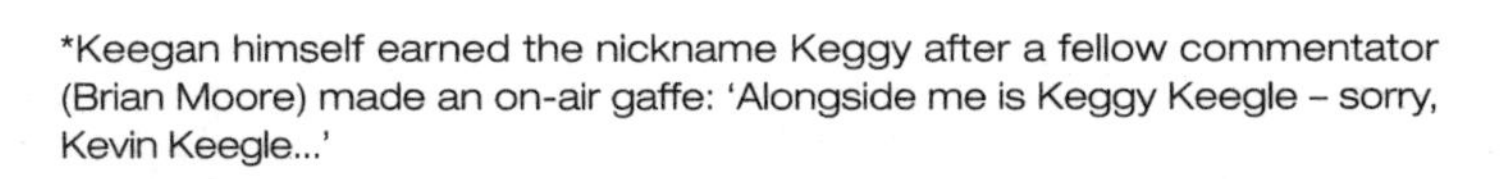

*Keegan himself earned the nickname Keggy after a fellow commentator (Brian Moore) made an on-air gaffe: 'Alongside me is Keggy Keegle – sorry, Kevin Keegle...'

In the English game, just about the only two who talk any sense are two Frenchmen, Arsene Wenger and Thierry Henry, Arsenal's manager and striker respectively. Wenger's intelligent post-match dissections are respected throughout the game and Henry, well, they say that he's the only football player who could ever talk a woman into bed...

footie-speak: an incomplete a–z

Warning: use these words and phrases with caution, or with a hint of irony. Only the real pros can use them in everyday speech without getting laughed at.

'All credit to the lads'
Usually uttered by the match scorer to modestly deflect the attention from himself. May or may not be coupled with 'delighted'.

'Couldn't score in a brothel with a £50 note tied to his chopper'
A term associated with a striker struggling to find the back of the net.

'Early doors'
A phrase much favoured by the 'late' Big Ron; if a team scores during the first few minutes of the time period they've

made a very good start to the game. No idea what the doors are referring to.

'I'm flattered by their interest but... '
Players use this phrase when they're linked with a move to another club. They'll be pulling on that club's shirt within days.

'Left peg'
Talented left-footed players are blessed with one of these, whereas right-footed players have 'feet'.

'Mixer'
The penalty area. As in 'stick it in the mixer'.

'Nutmeg'
A term used to describe a player kicking a ball between his opponent's legs. Often shortened to 'megs'.

'Onion bag'
Quite a poetic one, this. It refers to that thing that hangs off the crossbar, the net.

'Pop'
Often replaced nowadays by 'crack,' this term refers to having a shot from outside the box. Commentators often accompany it with 'it was always going over.'

'Quality'
Either 'shines through' or 'is sadly lacking.'

'Sleeping giant'
When clubs have high opinions of themselves but haven't actually won anything for years, this is how they're described.

'Showboating'
Showing off with fancy footwork. Christiano Ronaldo (Manchester United) does this a lot.

'Taking each game as it comes'
Or 'hoping for the best, but don't bet on us, eh?'

'Unfashionable club'
A small-town team.

'Very much so'
The Newcastle and ex-England striker Alan Shearer uses this a lot when he wants to string out sentences and appear more interesting. He should just use 'yes'.

'Wire'
The end. As in 'this could go to the wire' (often means 'please don't turn off before the ad break, it'll get better, it really will!')

'Y'know... '
Another favourite of Shearer's. He also refers to himself in

the third person ('Alan Shearer's a fighter... ') and that's just wrong.

'Row Z'

When defenders are in trouble, they have to kick the ball out of play and into the stands. Commentators then speculate whether they hoofed it out to 'row Z' – the farthest seats away.

6

Get tooled up for a tongue lashing...

how to win bar stool soccer debates

Men love nothing more than having alcohol-fuelled 'discussions' about football with their mates. Well, that's not strictly true, they love oral sex and roast potatoes a whole lot more, but footie debates really are right up there on their top ten list of leisure pursuits. Fortunately, they keep on going back to the same old handful of hackneyed arguments and never think to check the facts when they're sober. In this chapter you'll find all the ammunition you need to win some of the most common barstool battles. They won't like you for it, but then again, sometimes men need to be taught a lesson...

DEBATE

Which English club has won the most trophies?

definitive comeback

Liverpool.

the facts

Taking major trophies into account – League, FA Cup, League Cup, European Cup, Cup Winners' Cup and UEFA Cup – the Scousers have won 38 pieces of shiny hammered metal. This is nine more trophies than their nearest rivals, Manchester United, who have admittedly won the FA Cup four more times than their westerly counterparts. Sort of interestingly, Liverpool is not the most successful footballing city in England – London has more pieces of silverware in its collective club cabinets.

DEBATE

Wayne Rooney is the only player to have scored a hat-trick where all the goals were from outside the box.

definitive comeback

No he isn't.

the facts

At least four others have done it in recent years: Rivaldo, Sinisa Mihajlovic, David Farrell and Lee Johnson. Yeovil Town's Johnson did it in the 2004–05 season with two fantastic goals and one almighty stroke of luck. Farrell belted in three screamers for Peterborough versus Barnet in 2000, and Mihajlovic did it in style two years earlier by scoring from three free kicks in a 5–2 win over

Sampdoria. Rivaldo's hat-trick is the most respected though – he was playing for Barcelona against Valencia on the last day of the season in 2001. They were both in with a chance of a Champions' League place, so both teams really wanted to win at all costs. Twice Rivaldo put them into the lead but twice the Valencians equalised. Then, oh and then, he scored from 20 yards out with a perfectly executed overhead kick. The Barcelona fans were so chuffed it inspired the club's first and only pitch invasion.

DEBATE

You can't get booked without stepping onto the pitch.

definitive comeback

It happens quite often actually.

the facts

Former West Bromwich Albion player Enzo Maresca was shown a yellow card for celebrating a goal too enthusiastically from the subs bench, whereas goalkeeper Tim Flowers was once carded for abusing one of the match officials. The classic instance though was when, during the 2002 World Cup, Argentine player Claudio Caniggia was actually sent off for dissent (answering back to an official) during a match against Sweden. The midfielder was on the subs bench at the time, and his volley of petulant back-chat resulted in him not kicking a ball for his country for the duration of the competition. He also missed the 1998 World Cup through suspension.

DEBATE

Who are the only English team to have won all four divisions?

definitive comeback

Wolverhampton Wanderers and Burnley.

the facts

This is a perfect teaser for you to introduce into the conversation – unless they're Wolves or Burnley fans it's highly unlikely they'll know and they'll beg you for the answer all night. Which could work to your advantage...

Though they're hardly 'glamour' teams, Wolves and Burnley have indeed won every league there is to win, which is more than Sir Alex Ferguson's rabble can lay claim to. Wolves first won the title in 1954 and then in 1958 and 1959 (back-to-back winners, which is pretty nifty). But they've also won the Second (1931–2), the Third (1989), the Fourth (1988) and... the old Third Division North (1923–4). The mighty clarets became the second team in history to nail all four when they won the Fourth Division in 1991–92 – their journey started back in 1897–98, when they clinched the Second Division. Tell your man to stick that in his pipe and smoke it.

DEBATE

What's the most violent football match on record?

definitive comeback

The so-called 'Battle of Santiago'.

the facts

When this match was first shown on TV in 1962, BBC presenter David Coleman introduced it like this: 'Good evening. The game you are about to see is the most stupid, appalling, disgusting and disgraceful exhibition of football, possibly in the history of the game.' This World Cup game between hosts Chile and Italy had been stirred up beforehand by a

couple of Italian journos who'd described the host nation as a dump.

The first foul came within 12 seconds of kick off and then it all went crazy. An Italian was sent off but had to be dragged off the pitch by a group of policemen, while a Chilean player (a professional boxer's son) flattened one of his opponents, who then retaliated by kicking him in the neck. Another Italian was whacked in the nose and many more were felled by fouls before the final whistle. The referee Ken Aston later lamented: 'I wasn't reffing a football match, I was acting as an umpire in military manoeuvres.' Final score: Chile 2 Italy 0.

DEBATE

Which team has spent the longest in the top division?

definitive comeback

Erm, depends.

the facts

Arsenal have sat in the top flight for longest, having stayed there ever since they were first promoted back in 1919. On present form, it's reasonably safe to assume that they'll remain there for a few more years yet. But when it comes to the total number of seasons spent at the top, the award goes to Everton, who have spent 100 seasons in the loftiest league.

DEBATE

Has a referee ever changed his mind?

definitive comeback

Yes, quite a few times.

the facts

It may seem like a futile act when you see a player arguing with the ref as there's no way he's going to change his mind, no matter how sound the player's reasoning is. But the men in black do, from time to time, act upon what they've been told. During a Kuwait versus France match in the 1982 World Cup, the Kuwaiti players stopped dead after apparently hearing the ref's whistle. He had not blown, however, so the French kept on running towards goal and scored. And then they chuckled heartily at their good fortune. Their elation soon turned to anger, however, when the president of the Kuwaiti FA ran onto the pitch to give the Soviet referee a verbal 'seeing to', and the ref responded by disallowing the goal – having allowed it just seconds earlier.

Even the 'best ref in the world', Pierluigi Collina (bald chap, mad eyes – you know him), has submitted to on-pitch pressure. When Juventus played Internazionale in Italy a few years ago, Collina disallowed a goal purely on the strength of the opposition's moans that the scorer was offside. A video replay later proved that they (and he) were right in the end, but still.

DEBATE

Has a league or cup match ever been rigged?

definitive comeback

Definitely. Proving it's a different matter though.

the facts

The game that has raised more eyebrows than any other throughout history took place during the 1982 World Cup in Spain, when West Germany and Austria met in the final match in their group. If Germany won, both the (neighbouring countries) teams would make it through to the next round. After ten minutes German duly scored and the game simply ground to a halt. The players passed the ball between themselves and made virtually no attempts on goal for the remaining 80 minutes, despite the crowd's clear contempt for the whole affair. One German fan even burned a national flag in disgust. The last round of matches in many competitions are now played simultaneously.

Also worth considering is one further fishy match. To qualify for the finals of the 1984 European Championship, Spain needed to beat Malta by 11 clear goals. Now, Malta are admittedly rubbish, but seeing as Spain were winning by just 3–1 at half time, it was really unlikely they'd be able to score nine in the last 45 minutes. They blummin' well did though. Fancy that.

DEBATE

The best ever player was/is...

definitive comeback

WARNING: Getting into this argument without an extensive and lengthy knowledge of the game is potential suicide. When this one comes up in the pub, simply hold your hands up and repeat the following: 'There are so many different players and positions that it's impossible to measure success like that. Is a defender a better player than a striker because he's prevented more goals than that striker's scored? Judging on pure talent, I'd have to say Pele, Zidane or Maradona though. What do you think?' Then pull up a chair, nod and smile sweetly as your interrogator wraps himself up in knots.

7

Victoria's secrets...

learn to love the curious world of televised football

There's a hefty reference book that exists purely in men's heads called *Everything a Man Needs To Know About Watching Football On The Telly* that is filled with complex rules and regulations such as the following: 'Televised football etiquette dictates that upon entering a public house with a match in progress, spectators should squint and approach the big screen before ordering a drink or even acknowledging their associates. And they

should then refrain from exchanging salutations until a suitable break in the game.' Not being a man you'll never have to trawl through all that petty macho stuff, but there are a few simple guidelines to follow to aid your enjoyment of football on TV at home or in the pub. Or at least to prevent you from looking like a fool in public by offering to stick a song on the jukebox when a match goes to penalties.

There are two main differences between watching a live match and a game on the box: first, it's perfectly acceptable for anyone in the vicinity to wear a replica shirt (no matter what their size or shape, sadly). And second, you can drink alcohol while the action unfolds in front of you. This alters the atmosphere somewhat. Not the wearing-the-shirt bit, the booze bit.

preparation

Obviously, you'll have to go to the off licence if you are planning on drinking at home, but TV companies factor in time for this. The match always starts 15 minutes after the programme begins and no one really takes any notice of the punditry that goes on beforehand anyway. You'll want to see who's playing in which position though, and this happens about 45 seconds before kick off courtesy of an on-screen graphic.

If you're pub-bound, the website www.sportspubs.co.uk might be able to help you in your hunt for one that's showing the match, although it's always worth ringing ahead to find out which match they're planning on showing. More often than not you'll get through to a barman who is unaware if they even have a television. That said, there's not usually a choice (the same 'big' match will be shown all over the country), but sometimes – say, when Scotland and England are both playing at the same time – some bars will differ.

Get to the pub early. Not just because you'll want to bag a seat, but because the pre-match livener is as important as it is when watching a live game (reformed alcoholics may disagree, but they're just deluding themselves.) Naturally, lager is football's natural bedfellow, but it can test the bladder something rotten. Avoid frequent trips to the loo (and the bar/fridge) by getting a bottle of wine in.

It's a curious thing, but only the most fanatical of fans – they're *not* the ones with tattoos of spiders' webs over their faces, they're the ones who look like IT support technicians in football shirts – discuss the match beforehand. Someone might offer up a score but that's about as far as it goes. This is because it's all too easy to make a fool of yourself with a rash opinion that can be proved wrong very publicly within the next hour and a half. It's far safer to praise or criticise after the event.

So, you've got yourself sat down with a clear view of the action and beside someone you can have a natter with, there's an uncorked Pinot Grigio in front of you, the team position graphic is up ('no surprises there then' is a handy phrase to bandy about at this stage) and you're ready for kick off. Been to the loo yet? Thought not.

kick off

Whether you're watching in the pub or at home, the volume has got to be loud. Stadium loud, if the TV can manage it. This isn't to make out the commentary from the sheepskin-coated men bleating into their microphones from way up in the stands, however. God no, they're only any good when it comes to explaining how many goals have to be scored and saved during penalty shootouts (it's really very simple, but after a few vinos and a fraught match the brain can turn to mush). No, you need it loud to get the rumble, the cheers and – frankly – the insults emanating from the stadium.

International matches are best for picking up the aural atmosphere. If you're watching a Spain game, listen out for the big bass drum of Monsieur La Bomba. He's a swarthy chap who leads the crowd in their chanting. (Pedants please note: it is not known why he's not called *Señor* la Bomba, seeing as he's Spanish, but there's not a lot that can be done about that.)

Similarly, there are a bunch of England fans who insist on following the team all over the planet and playing the theme from the *Great Escape* on brass instruments. And that gets very annoying. There is some entertainment to be had from hearing England supporters however, as they swear like sailors with the clap. It's childish, but there's nothing better than hearing: '*He's fat, he's Scouse, he'll rob your f*cking house, it's*

Wayne Rooney, Wayne Rooney,' in the background when the commentator's droning on about 'the side of English football we don't want to see.'

Visually speaking, there's a load of stuff to look out for when the game gets a bit boring. Indeed, the programme makers will do their best to bring the viewers at least one of the following in every match:

- A busty Brazilian girl in her national kit laughing and perhaps doing some samba dancing.
- A goggle-eyed nerd standing next to the aforementioned samba dancer who can't believe his luck.
- A child looking despondent: 'And there's one little lad who'll be crying at bedtime tonight' or...
- A child looking gleeful: 'Look at that little chap, he's having a whale of a time, bet he'll remember tonight for the rest of his life.'
- A couple of chaps who only realise that they're being filmed when one of them spots the in-stadium monitors. They'll then gurn for the cameras and start saying something but the cameras will cut to someone else before you can work out what on earth it was they were going on about.
- A grown man crying.
- Someone famous looking glum (more often than not this will be Posh Spice).

In fact, keeping an eye out for any of the above can make for a welcome diversion or even a half-decent drinking game. Drain a glass of something suitably alcoholic every time you see one of the above, or down a row of five shots if a (male) streaker runs onto the pitch. Should a player wrestle that streaker to the ground (and curiously, they often choose to), you also have to sink a cocktail of your choice.

That's assuming the game's duff of course. Even if it's not, you're under no obligation to give the screen your undivided attention 100 per cent of the time; it's perfectly acceptable to have a natter to your mates and pop off to the bar from time to time. But, *Everything a Man Needs To Know About Watching Football On The Telly* dictates that you shall not nip to the toilet no matter how desperate you are and that you must keep one eye on the screen at all times. The only exception to this rule is when you're actually in the process of ordering a drink, you are then permitted to look directly at the barman – especially if he's gorgeous. Bear in mind, though, you'll pay for this because someone will score the moment you look away from the match, that's just what happens. All is not lost though, as one of the major benefits of watching football on the telly is the action replays.

A word about action replays: they *must* be respected. If you were to question the clients coming out of a divorce lawyer's, whereas most of the women would give the reason for the break up of their marriage as: 'we don't communicate,' most of the men would surely say: 'she kept on talking to me during replays.' They're that important. Football is a game that's usually high on action but low on goals, and goals are what everyone wants to see. If one of your team scores, you get an initial adrenaline rush, followed by a weaker second hit when you marvel at the replay. Talk during that replay and it's like withdrawing drugs from a junkie. It's slightly different in the pub because everyone will be making such a commotion from when the goal was first scored that the replay will be missed, but at home it's imperative that you wait until the ball has hit the back of the net before you shriek 'get in!' The exception to this rule is when one of the opposition scores, of course; if that happens you can scream at the screen all you like.

half time

Half time in the pub is like an interval at the theatre; everyone rushes to the bar or to the toilet (or, unlike the theatre, to the car park to score drugs or steal car stereos). Some enterprising pub chains have begun putting out order forms on the tables during major competitions so that you can order your drinks in advance, but if you've done your groundwork and given that gorgeous barman the eye in the first half you shouldn't have to wait too long for service.

Don't talk about the first half during half time, no one else does. The done thing is to clap your hands together at the half time whistle and say: 'Right, who fancies a drink?' It's also a good opportunity to do a circuit of the pub in search of decent looking men. Alternatively, if you're at home, don't continue watching the television thinking that the content will be anything like as exciting as it was. 15 minutes is a short time when it comes to going to the fridge, feeding the cat, having a wee and opening another bag of Kettle Chips, but it's a very long time in the land of football punditry.

The pundits differ from the commentators in that they are paid to give opinions before, during and after the match. Whereas the commentators have to appear to be neutral (even when a national side is playing), the pundits can come out with whatever nonsense they care to drunkenly string together. And, being ex-players and managers, they usually do. What makes it worse is that they've recently learned that to ensure that they get rebooked by the TV companies they've got to give value for money – this usually means being as controversial as they possibly can. Just ignore them and go and get stuck into those crisps. Or, even better, if you have any mates who support the losing team, take the Mickey out of them by text. Oh, and don't forget to have a wee.

back to the action

During live matches, chats about anything other than the events unfolding on the pitch are met with abject hostility by those within earshot. The same is true of games watched in the pub, but to a lesser extent. For example, here is how a typical non-footie-related conversation will go between two chaps (it should be noted that neither will take their eyes off the screen at any stage):

'Saw your missus last night.'
(20 second pause)
'Did you?'

(20 second pause)
'Yeah.'
(20 seconds pause)
'Where was she?'
(20 second pause)
'Shagging your next door neighbour in a shop doorway.'
(20 second pause)
'DID YOU SEE THAT F*CKING GOAL! GET IN! YOU BEAUTY!'
'Beckham's a f*cking legend!'
(20 second pause)
'What was that you were saying?'
(20 second pause)
'Can't remember.'

Naturally, this sort of stilted communication is macho bonkers, but it's the sort of restraint you should be aiming for if you want to avoid being told to 'shut the hell up'. A man's reluctance to chat during a game can also be a blessing though. If you ever need anything from your man (a promise that he'll take you out soon, a loan 'til pay day, that sort of thing), the best time to ask is when the match is on; he'll agree to anything just to get a bit of peace and quiet.

However, what you miss out on in girly gossip during a match, you can make up for in shoutin' and swearin'. There are precious few occasions when you can holler the F-word in a public place and get away with it – why, there are even fewer instances where people will actually nod their heads in agreement at your Tourretes-style outbursts. Knock yourself out: swear like you're the Top Dog in Holloway Prison.

For that's the key to enjoying a televised match, whether you're watching it in the pub or at home: passion. Get as carried away as if you were there in the stadium itself. Force yourself to shout, scream, swear or sigh with every kick of the game and you'll soon learn to love the curious world of televised football.

cautionary tip

One final thing: when watching football in the pub, you may feel compelled to flash your boobs (especially if your team's won) at the assembled crowd. This is normal, but it's probably best to resist the impulse – the popularity of camera phones means that your drunken moment of liberation will probably come back to haunt you.

8

Pitch bitch...

going to a live game

Every week, thousands of football fans take time off work, drive hundreds of miles and then stand in draughty stadiums, only to get back in the car and make their way home a couple of hours later. Often while wearing home-knitted hats and bad anoraks. Why do they do it? For the chance of the 20-second mass orgasm that follows when their team scores, that's why. Just as a slice of 'Be Good To Thyself' chocolate cake doesn't quite hit the spot in the same way as a double helping of 'Extra Special' pud, lager-drenched post-goal celebrations in the pub don't compare to the mass euphoria of the terraces, when, for a few short moments, thousands share exactly the same feelings of joy, exhilaration and triumph, while being able to whoop as loudly as drunken housewives at an Ann Summers party.

getting hold of tickets

You can find out when and where your boys are playing by consulting their fixture list, and the easiest way of doing this is by logging onto the BBC Sport website (tap 'fixtures', 'your team's name' and 'BBC' into Google and you'll get there). If only it were that easy to get hold of the tickets themselves. There are several factors that can complicate the process, but at its simplest your transaction should break down like this:

First, visit your club's official website or give the ticket office a ring; they'll then inform you if they've got any seats left and which 'category' the match comes under. There are usually three or four of these categories, which relate to how bankable your opponents are; a game against a European side might be category A, whereas a cup match versus a team from a lower league than yours would be category C.

Just to make things more complicated, ticket prices are further governed by where you sit – the most expensive seats are towards the front of the stands near the half-way line (because you can see both ends), and the cheapest are way up in the gods behind the goalkeepers. Make your selection and the club will pop the tickets in the post. That's the theory anyway.

However, if the match you want to see fulfils two or more of the criteria opposite, you may as well begin formulating a high-fat-high-carbs-no-excercise diet – you'll probably have greater success:

- Your team's Manchester United (or, to a lesser extent, any other Premiership club)
- You want tickets for this week's game
- It's the first/last fixture of the season
- It's a derby match (i.e. against the local rivals)
- You want tickets for Boxing Day.

In these instances, priority goes to official supporters' club members, so you'll have to get that sorted out first – the ticket office will be able to put you in touch with them – *and then* you may well have to go into a ballot. If your name's selected you can buy the tickets; if not, you'll have to look elsewhere. This usually means contacting a ticket agency (such as Ticketmaster.co.uk), or even the opposing team and seeing if they've got any tickets going begging in their 'end' of the stadium (away teams are allocated a number of seats in a segregated area away from the home fans). Obviously, if they come up trumps, you'll have to be reheeeally careful not to cheer your team or wear their colours, as the supporters might look at you funny. Or even throw coins at you. Then again, if you're that desperate you might be better off loitering outside the gates on match day and seeing if the, ahem, ticket touts have got anything (don't worry, they'll approach you). This is both expensive and illegal of course and not recommended.

Once you've got the tickets that really is the tricky bit over and done with. Except... WHAT IN THE NAME OF DJEMBA-DJEMBA* ARE YOU GOING TO WEAR?!

*Eric Djemba-Djemba is a bizarrely named Aston Villa player.

what to wear

Strictly speaking, you should dress yourself for a match according to the clichéd advice that your dad would have once doled out, advice such as: 'wrap up warm, it's cold out,' 'it's not a fashion parade' or even: 'I'm not giving you a lift in my car wearing *that*.' But, you probably didn't listen to him then, so there's no reason to start now.

You may have noticed that Posh and other assorted footballers' wives turn up to games in Chanel suits, strappy Blahniks and Gucci shades. There's a reason for that: they're whisked straight from the deserted staff car park to the lavish directors' box with its under-floor heating, plush carpeting and gold-plated coat hangers. You, however, will be jostled by the lumpen proletariat through the turnstiles through the scrum of the terraces to your seat, which will lean back at an alarming angle of 20 degrees, giving spectators on the opposite side of the stadium a magnificent view of between your legs. So, unless exhibitionism floats your boat, you might want to forgo a skirt.

Additionally, you'll want to resist the impulse to don your

team's shirt. No one looks good in football shirts, apart from footballers, naturally. Contrary to popular belief, not all fans wear the latest season's shirt; they only tend to be worn by a hardcore of fanatics, nutters, children, and men seemingly in their third trimester of pregnancy who only break into a sweat when lifting a full pint to their lips. Wear one about the house, or in bed as treat for your boyf, but never to a match (with the exception of international games or the finals of a competition, when every man, woman and child in the stadium has to do their duty). Besides, no woman should wear that much nylon as a matter of course; the static generated from the plastic can ruin a hairstyle in seconds. If you have to acknowledge your allegiance to the team, less is much, much more.

So, jeans, combats or tight trousers are good and, bearing in mind that it's chuffing cold in this country for 80 per cent of the season, your best bet is to team them up with a top – not a 'booby' top, you'll spill out with every goal celebration and you'll still be thawing out your nipples by the time of the next match – and a coat. An urban look is what you should be aiming for – practical but sexy at the same time.

As we all know, football grounds are literally crammed to the rafters with MEN. And even if none of the players float your boat, picking out a good-looking stud is easy. The reason for this is that, because the men who go to matches don't expect to pull, they make no effort at all with their appearance. They'll not bother combing their hair or cleaning their teeth and turn up in all manner of fashion disasters: football shirts, fleeces, rubbish jeans and even home-knits.

This behaviour acts as a natural man-filter; those who can be arsed to make themselves look decent even at a football match are likely to be worth some attention.

As for footwear: go booted up. A pair of boots, preferably with a heel, will help you assert your position in the terrace scrum and fend off unwanted advances from pregnant men. Bear in mind though that the higher your heels, the greater your chances of trudging home barefoot with your boots slung over your shoulder.

getting there

OK, say the kick off's at three o'clock, it should take you half an hour to get to the stadium, and 15 minutes should be enough to get through the turnstiles and find your seat, so you can leave your place at two o'clock and still have plenty of time to nip into a nail bar and go back and change your boots because you've broken a heel, right? Wrong. You've overlooked a) the pre-match opener, and b) the aggravation factor of thousands of other fans piling into the area at the last minute.

the opener

Having a couple of jars prior to the match is as traditional as having sex with an unsuitable colleague at the staff Christmas bash. Why, at one time you could buy grog at stadiums. The authorities were forced to ban alcohol when the game turned a bit hooligany back in the 80s, but football and booze remain firm friends. Generally speaking, the nearer you are to the stadium, the busier (and rougher) the pub'll be, so you might want to choose a bar a bit further away. A sign on the window that says: 'NO AWAY FANS' is a sure sign that the landlord has to keep a chainsaw under the bar for protection, but a 'SORRY, NO FOOTBALL SHIRTS' notice is a welcome one that roughly translates into: 'COME IN! PREGNANT MAN FREE ZONE.' Get a couple of drinks down you – lager, cider or wine, *not* a spritzer or a Cosmopolitan cocktail – sample the menu if you wish (it's really not worth holding out for the stadium catering as you'll find out in a few pages), but don't get so trolleyed that you can't walk in a straight line or the stewards won't let you into the ground.

seating issues

You need to get to the stadium around 30 minutes before kick off. This will give you time to queue at the gates, peruse the overpriced tat in the club shop, ignore the programme vendors (club programmes are pretty dire) and clean yourself up after slipping on one of the half-eaten burgers that are invariably strewn around the fast food vendors' vans. On your ticket should be a turnstile number and a seat code; simply find the turnstile, hand over your ticket to the attendant and try and walk through without catching your handbag in the mechanism. You'll then be faced with a raft of steps and, as you climb these, a number of doors through which men can quite clearly be seen either a) acting like braying yahs in the hospitality suite, or b) urinating into each others pockets, the sinks or the urinals depending on how busy it is. Your seating area should be signposted, but if not, seek out one of the stewards (they wear fluorescent jackets and loiter in the aisles smoking and chatting to their mates).

Unless you're extremely lucky, you'll be sat in the middle of a row and will probably have to cut a swathe through a line of grumbling old men to reach your place. On the way you might see name plaques on some of the seats; these are *not* to commemorate dead fans, they're seats reserved for season ticket holders. This is the only concession season ticket holders get towards exclusivity though, as the seats are miserably uncomfortable wherever you get plonked. The crotch-displaying angle is bad enough, but – if you're taller than five feet – the lack of legroom is a killer. Footie clubs make their cash by selling tickets to watch the game, obviously, and it follows that the smaller the seat, the greater the number of paying spectators they can cram into the stands. As such, there's no opportunity for canny cinema-style-pass-me-the-popcorn manoeuvres to bag extra arm room. You and your neighbour have to come to an unspoken arrangement and stick with it until half time at least. The arrangement that works best is whereby one of you leans back in the seat and the other leans forward so that your torsos are staggered, allowing both your ribcages room to expand naturally, thereby facilitating breathing. If not, you risk a mouth-to-mouth encounter with a moustachioed (either sex) St John Ambulance volunteer, and that's never nice.

mixing it

Unfortunately, seeing as matches are public events, you'll have to mix it with some 'colourful characters'. Every stand of every club in the land has more than its fair share of loons who turn up week in week out and are seemingly on nodding terms with everyone. They tend to fall into one of three categories: the geriatric oldsters who grumble, stink of wee and wear football scarves that date back to the 1940s; foul-mouthed, chain-smoking, fur coat-wearing hags who tell everyone that they could make a better job of managing the team; and middle-aged bachelors who sport quirky headwear (a red trilby avec feather, for instance) and smoke slim cheroots. This assortment of mentalists is also backed up by a sprinkling of supporters who fancy themselves as pundits and pollute the airspace with a running commentary of the events on the pitch. Avoid.

Happily, not all spectators are one stud short of a boot. In fact, you'll be surprised at how many of your seated neighbours engage you in genuinely innocent conversation. That's the beauty of watching a live match; the fact that you're sat with other people who follow the same team means that you're automatically adjudged to be 'alright', and because you're virtually perched on someone else's lap, it's churlish not to acknowledge their presence or point out what a twonk someone on the field is being. These polite exchanges aren't driven by romantic intention, but there's nothing in the rules to say you can't exploit the situation if your new terrace chum just happens to look like George Clooney. Simply strike up a conversation by confessing that you're losing your live match cherry and await the inevitable response.

the warm up

Once seated, your eyes will no doubt be drawn to the pitch. The first thing you'll notice is that it looks tiny, the second thing you'll spot is a clutch of wobbly teenage girls wearing tan tights and sparkly leotards, leaping about to a disco track from the 1970s. Yes, they're cheerleaders, but – if you watch them for more than a minute – you'll notice they're nowhere near as good as their American counterparts. They're invariably crap, in fact. It's best to ignore them; they'll go away in a minute.

You can also pay no heed to any other forms of 'razzmatazz' that the club has laid on for your entertainment. The guy on

the PA is probably on loan from Radio Lollipop and will be trying to fulfil his quota of match sponsor mentions by way of a 'wacky' game, and the club mascot – usually a shabby cartoon critter – will no doubt be doing cartwheels and falling on his face a lot. Occasionally, though, he might get involved in a tussle with an opposing mascot. Two grown men in foam outfits trying to lay each other out does make for surprisingly good entertainment, but the clubs don't encourage this sort of behaviour in front of the young fans.

Also on the pitch will be a few of the home team's apprentices. They'll be shamelessly showboating their silky skills in front of the assembled throng, but trying to pass it off as a casual kick-about. Do not encourage these little oiks by cheering their keepy-uppy shenanigans – save yourself for the pros, who'll be on in a tick. In fact, now's a good time to nip to the loo, as to do so during the action is as about as socially acceptable as eating dolphin meat sandwiches on the Tube. You'll be pleased to learn that, because women are very much in the minority at football stadiums, you won't have to queue for a cubicle.

you what?

You'll probably be relieved to discover that you're not morally obliged to shout and cheer for the duration of the game. Some fans do, and they can generally be found in the cheaper seats. Each and every spectator is, however, party to a baffling series of cheers, shouts and groans that punctuate the various peculiar incidents that are thrown up by the game – think of the audience participation at a live performance of the Rocky Horror Show (with a lot less transvestism, obviously) and you're on the right lines. These are in addition to the usual post-goal celebrations and the missed-goal groans, and it's not quite clear how everyone knows just what noise to make and when, they just do. If you want to avoid looking like an atheist who's mistakenly turned up to a recording of Songs Of Praise, you'll need to swot up on the following:

yay (times eleven)

The hospital DJ will read out the day's team sheet before they run onto the pitch. He'll start with the home team first; if they're not your boys, remain mute. After he announces each member of your team it's customary to offer a little cheer. The 'yays' will get progressively quieter as he reaches players number nine, ten and eleven, but once he's completed the line-up you're obliged to clap and cheer the team as a whole.

manon!

Literally 'man on', this is used to warn one of your players that he is about to be tackled from behind (when he hasn't spotted his would-be assailant). Shouting this makes the supporters feel as if they're directly contributing to the game, but it's more of a 'he's behind you' pantomime cry really.

yay (repeated)

If play gets a bit dull and your boys take to pointlessly passing the ball between themselves for a bit, the supporters will offer a little 'yay' and a chuckle for every completed pass. They'll stop when the opposition takes possession, naturally. Once this has happened once, your team will probably try it again (they like the attention), before getting back to the business of scoring goals.

amball!/'fside!

If one of your opponents touches the ball with his arm or hand or is caught offside, it's up to you to bring it to the attention of the ref by shouting 'amball!' or 'fside!' respectively (handball and offside). You can raise one of your hands at the same time if you like – you'll notice that most of your players will be doing the same.

waaaaayyyyy...

Very rarely heard, this gentle groan is brought into play if the floodlights fail. Everyone does it, no one knows why.

aayy

When a ball is inadvertently booted into the stands, spectators are almost obliged to try and head it back into play. If the individual who connects with the ball succeeds in doing this, everyone gives him a bit of recognition for his efforts. If he or she is caught out and ends up being knocked senseless by the shot, supporters are morally obliged to laugh at his buffoonery. Note: if the ball comes your way, don't try and keep it as they do in baseball matches – you'll be admonished by your fellow supporters. That said, if your team is desperately holding onto a one-goal lead with only a couple of minutes until the final whistle, you may take your time about punting it back onto the pitch.

wooooohh...

When a keeper has to make a goal kick (see chapter four), his run up may well be accompanied by the wooooohh... sound. It will go on for as long as it takes to kick the ball, which can be some time if he's one that likes to clear bits of scrub from his path and cross himself beforehand. If it's their keeper that's taking the kick, some of your fellow supporters may well round off the wooooohh... with 'you're shit ahhhhh!', which is always nice.

(silence)

When someone scores during a British televised match, the director will either cut to a shot of the crowd going utterly mental or the scorer doing the same. Never will the camera pan along the faces of the fans of the team that's just conceded the goal. There's a reason for that: absolutely nothing happens. It's different if the goal is contentious (if the player was offside or knocked it in with his hand, say), but if not, simply file your emotions under 'good sportsmanship' and look to the centre spot with assured dignity.

half time

You'll know when half time's coming because the terrace lighting, which is dimmed soon after kick off, is switched back on again. This is presumably done to accommodate the aged male punters whose prostrates can't manage a full 45 minutes without peeing, and gastronomic mentalists who can't wait to get their hands on the stadium catering. However, unless you like either flash-fried or boiled reconstituted animal products wrapped in various forms of heavy stodge, you might like to use the precious fifteen-minute break to visit the loo, exercise away the early symptoms of deep vein thrombosis or have a fag (note: smoking during the match itself is frowned upon because you're penned in so close to your neighbours).

Generally speaking, the catering within football grounds is abysmal, overpriced and served so slowly that you'll miss most of the second half. Bizarrely, almost every club dishes up lava-hot pies (heavy on the kidney, easy on the steak), which are about as easy to eat with your bare hands as live elvers, and some still serve hot beefy drinks – the desire for animal product in all its forms runs strong within football fans. Note: deviating from the menu by asking for an ingredient to be left out, added or substituted will result in a stereophonic torrent of abuse from the kitchen staff and those in the queue behind you.

FYI: In 1998, the now defunct *Colman's Football Food Guide* produced a league table of the catering facilities at soccer grounds throughout England and Wales. The study found some horror stories, including a kebab that contained a maggot, a burger with a fingernail and a pie that apparently tasted like dog food. Cambridge United came top of the league, and Norwich City – where Delia Smith is a director – came 61st.

back to the action

Once the managers have given their boys a bollocking (managers always dole out bollockings, no matter how well the team played in the first half) and passed around the isotonic sports drinks, he'll send them back out for the second instalment. You might've missed their entrance prior to the first half, but you'll notice that the teams run on under the cover of a collapsible canopy that extends well onto the pitch itself. This is so that the crowd can't spit at them. It's interesting to note that when they come out for the second half, they emerge from the tunnel like dogs with their tails on fire. This could be for one of two reasons: a) they played really well in the first half and want to get the job done or b) they played really badly and are conscious of the fact that many of the spectators are now armed with pastry products filled with napalm-like contents.

Anyhow, the second half'll be much like the first apart from the fact that if your team's on the end of a right stuffing, all your fellow fans will abandon hope, become mournfully quiet and begin counting down the minutes until they can make a run for their cars without looking like deserters. Strictly speaking, real fans shouldn't leave before the ref blows up for the end of the game, especially not at a home fixture. Besides, would you leave a cinema five minutes before the end of a film? Of course not, you might miss the best bit. This is precisely what happened to George Best when he left the Champions League Final in Barcelona in 1999, with Manchester United a goal down in injury time. The Red Devils duly slotted in two goals in the dying seconds and won the most prestigious trophy in European football while ex-United player Bestie was in the car park cranking up his motor. It's also worth noting that, unlike at other spectator events, no matter how bad it gets, none of them will fall asleep. This is because if you get spotted having a snooze in the company of a few thousand others, you could be arrested for being drunk at a football ground, which is a criminal offence (as a Middlesbrough fan found to his cost in 2002 during his team's 4–0 defeat against Arsenal).

final whistle

At the end of the game the stadium will empty quicker than a crate of Bacardi Breezers at a hen night. There's a simple reason for this: everyone wants to get to the pub. The general form is to follow the herd with a neutral expression regardless of your team's performance or the result – shouting something like 'you beauties!' and punching the air is just not done. (Unless it's a really big match, in which case you are entitled to holler all you like and, if the opportunity presents itself, bare your bum to passing motorists.) However, this swift mass exodus does provide an excellent opportunity for man spotting, though striking up a conversation before you get out of the stadium environs and into the 'real world' of bumbling social interaction is somewhat challenging.

Thankfully, football violence is generally a thing of the past – except for the occasional flare up at local derbies – and if there's any sign of trouble, the police will escort opposing fans from the stadium separately. Not that you need the protection of course, simply being a woman prevents you from getting a thumping. Granted, some men aren't averse to beating up women, but if they dared try it in the street, supporters from both teams would lynch them. The only thing you have to worry about is what you're going to order in the pub. Yes – the post-match livener is equally as important as the pre-match opener.

Once safely ensconced within licensed premises or, if it's an away match, the confines of the car, then and only then can you begin the delicious dissection of the night's performance with your mates. But don't get too comfy. You have to get back in time for the highlights to see if you can spot yourself on telly – woo-hoo!

9

'We've all had your missus' and other chants that would horrify your mother

When England were humiliatingly defeated 1–0 by Germany in the final match at the old Wembley stadium in 2002, the German supporters took to their feet and treated their opponents to a chorus of '*You're sh*t and you know you are*', in English. It might not be the most lyrically intricate put-down of all time, but for the Germans to use it then, in their opponent's national stadium, in their own language, made it deliciously withering.

Chants are hurled across every terrace of every stadium of every country in the football-loving world and each nation has their own idiosyncratic way of voicing their opinions. Whereas the Germans seemingly favour cruel irony, the Spanish come out with songs that are supposed to inspire their players and the Turks have sing-a-longs about how much they'd like to rip out and eat the still-beating hearts of the opposition. Most of the time though, British fans just take the mickey out of each other. And that's a big part of what makes watching football so much fun.

Some academics from the University of Liverpool came up with a rather long-winded mathematical formula for the perfect chant ahead of the 2004 European Championships. They determined that – and bear with it – fans should multiply contribution (C) by intensity (I) and divide it by aggression (A). They should then add the measure of performance in adversity (P), which should then be multiplied by the sum of spontaneity (S) and humour (H). The final calculation required was the amount of topicality (T) squared (the equation looks like this, if you're interested: $[C \times I/A] + P(S + H) + T^2$). However, the number-crunchers needn't have bothered going to all that trouble, as any fan could have told them that the best chants are simply funny and cutting; that's all there is to it.

Of course, as a quick think about the people you work

with will confirm, lots of people think they're funny when in reality they're as humorous as a bikini wax. This is why, if you fancy starting your own chant off – and you can, anyone at a match can start a chant and if people like it it'll quickly get taken up by the whole crowd – you should stop and think *really* hard. It's shockingly embarrassing if no one joins in or laughs – just try and sing along with everyone else for your first few matches.

What your fellow stadium-dwellers will sing about is anyone's guess. Chants change as the events on the pitch unfold, and you won't know what on Earth they're on about at first, but stick with it and you'll soon pick it up. You'll notice that no one mouths silently or mumbles along like they used to during hymns at harvest festival. This is not because everyone but you has attended a top secret football chanting school, it's because they're easier than nursery rhymes to learn. There are hundreds of ways of winding up the opposition, but generally speaking, you'll taunt your opponents about their footballing ineptitude (*'Can we play you every week?'*); pick on their players (*'Who ate all the pies?'*); ridicule their regional accents (*'We speak English over here'*); poke fun at their local customs (*'What's it like to shag a sheep?'*) or just be extremely rude about their hospitality (*'Shall we buy a ground for you?'*).

In fact, over the years there have been some superb examples of the razor wit found on the terraces. The following are the stuff of footballing legend (and if you can remember them, they'll impress your man no end):

'We were watching the Bill – what was the score in Seville?'
This is what Rangers fans sang to their arch-rivals Celtic after they returned home empty-handed from the 2003 UEFA Cup Final in Spain.

'Is that all she gets at home?
Is that all she gets at home?'
Chanted by Chelsea fans to a male streaker at an away FA Cup tie versus Shrewsbury in 2003.

'Neville Neville, they're in defence,
Neville Neville , their future's immense.
Neville Neville, they ain't half bad,
Neville Neville, the name of their dad.'
(Sung to the tune of David Bowie's '*Rebel Rebel*'.) This is what the two footballing brothers, Gary and Philip Neville, have to put up with every time they take to the pitch. Their dad's first name really is Neville, though.

'We've all had your missus.
We've all had your missus'
This is the reason you must never agree to go on the pitch at half time if you suspect your boyfriend may be about to propose.

'There's only one Sally Gunnell'
Often aimed at Villarreal striker Diego Forlan. He does look a hell of a lot like her.

But when fans are not taking the mickey out of each other, they're getting all misty-eyed and devotional about their club or their country. Every club has a roster of a dozen songs or so that everyone in the stadium learns every line of – seemingly by osmosis – and each week at least one of these ditties is sung in full. With gusto. Liverpool are one of the best-known clubs for crooning, they're famed for '*You'll Never Walk Alone*,' but they've more songs in their repertoire than are in a hymn book. Here's just a snatch of a particularly vomit-inducing ditty they yodel in honour of current hero, Steven Gerard.

(To the tune of *Let It Be*)
'When we find ourselves in times of trouble,
Stevie G runs past me,
Playing the game with wisdom, Stevie G,
And in my home, the Spion Kop,
We watch him jog, right in front of me,
Spreading balls with wisdom, Stevie G...'

Dodgy, isn't it? '*Spreading balls with wisdom*' indeed...

You'll note that the above verse was to a Beatle's melody, and that's not unusual, but if you're ever in doubt of the tune behind a chant, go with the old Cuban hit

Guantanamera, which is used in the majority of cases. For example, three of the five most commonly heard chants are based on it:

'One team in (place name). There's only one team in (place name)...'

'Sing when you're winning. You only sing when you're winning..'

'One (player's name). There's only one (player's name)...'

And the other two most-sung terrace standards are sung to the tune of a lovely old hymn called *Guide Me O Thou Great Redeemer* (er, you'll know it when you hear it):

*'Who's the w*nker?*
*Who's the w*nker?*
*Who's the w*nker in the black?'*
(The 'w*nker' is the referee, by the way.)

'You're not singing.
You're not singing.
You're not singing any more'
(Shout this when the opposition are losing and have gone quiet.)

It is estimated that there are over 10,000 different football chants in the UK, but as long as you can remember the aforementioned five, the rest'll come easily. If you really want to go as far as learning a few chants before a particular match, visit www.footballchants.org, where there are the lyrics to just about every song sung by every supporter in Britain.

Don't print them off and take them with you to a match though, that's even more excruciatingly embarrassing than starting off a chant that no one wants to join in with.

10

Studs and stilettos...

women's football

Football is the top female sport in the UK and over 100,000 women and girls regularly pull on their sports bras and studded boots for organised kick-abouts (though not all at the same time, that would be a logistical nightmare). This might seem like a pretty impressive turnout, but if the women's game hadn't been banned outright in its early days, there would be so many more players now.

In 1921 the Football Association issued the following decree: '... the Council feel impelled to express their strong opinion that the game of football is unsuitable for females and ought not to be encouraged... the Council request clubs belonging to the Association to refuse the use of their grounds for such matches.' The supposedly wise and presumably bearded men of the FA took this ludicrous course of action after 53,000 turned up to watch a women's match played at Everton's ground, because they were apparently fearful that its popularity would detract from the men's game. Thankfully, things have changed.

The FA's previously retrograde attitude to females kicking bits of inflated leather about is in keeping with several other male-centric 'organisations' throughout history. It was the Chinese Qing Dynasty of 1644 that first banned women from playing footie – despite the fact that the first known records of the game are murals of women having a kickabout during the Chinese Donghan Dynasty (AD 25–220) – and both the German and Dutch football associations imposed similar restrictions during the 1950s.

It wasn't until two decades later that women's football began really taking off on a global scale. Italy, Denmark, Sweden and Norway pioneered the sport at first, but the Japanese, the Brazillians and the hirsute German frauleins all now boast strong teams. In fact, Germany are the current European and World Champions.

Of course, the Americans, who have the resources to throw huge sums of cash at whatever they fancy, have also flourished. They've won the World Cup twice and also took the first ever Olympic gold for women's football in 1996. In fact, the players of the American national team were the first women to be paid on a full-time professional basis, and players from the (now sadly defunct) Women's United Soccer Association League could demand six-figure sponsorship deals.

at home

Ironically, the FA – who banned women's football back in the bad old days – have been in charge of the game in England since 1993 and it's now flourishing under their stewardship. Before they took over there were only 80 girls' teams, but today they claim 'there are over 3,500, and an estimated 45,000 under-16 players. There are 42 Girls' Centres of Excellence (mainly linked to men's clubs), 20 academies and a fully-funded scholarship programme for elite England players at Loughborough University'. There are Under-21, Under-19 and Senior sides at national level, and they've set themselves an ambitious target: winning the Women's World Cup in 2007. And under the current manager, they might just do it.

HOPE POWELL OBE

Hope Powell is a heroine of English women's football, if not the game as a whole. She was made the first ever full-time National Coach of the women's team in June 1998, having honed her skills as an experienced international who boasts 66 caps for England (and an equally impressive 35 goals). She first played footie with Millwall Lionesses at the age of 11 and has lifted the women's FA cup three times, including the league and cup double as captain of Croydon in 1996. As a coach, Hope became the first woman to achieve the UEFA Pro Licence – the highest coaching award available – and her achievements to date include taking the Under-19s to the semi-finals of the 2002 and 2003 UEFA Women's Championship and to the quarter-finals of the first ever FIFA U19 World Championship in 2002. Watch your back Sven.

Unlike, say, tennis, where women play a pared down version of the men's game, the rules are exactly the same in women's football. There are only a few differences between the styles of play on the pitch (the game is slightly slower and there's a bit less chesting of the ball in women's footie) and the major competitions even sound the same as the men's – woo-hoo! There are the European Championships and the Women's World Cup (both held every four years) for national squads, and in England the competitions are:

- The FA Nationwide Women's Premier League (National, Northern and Southern Divisions)
- The FA Women's Cup

- The FA Premier League Cup
- The FA Women's Community Shield.

There are only ten teams in the Premier League at present and in recent years Arsenal have dominated – much the same as in the men's game. The top flight is somewhat different from the (men's) Premiership, however, as it contains teams such as Bristol Rovers and Doncaster Rovers who can usually be found languishing in much lower divisions. The squads currently in the FA Nationwide Women's Premier League are:

- Everton Ladies
- Charlton Women
- Leeds Utd Ladies
- Bristol Rovers Women
- Arsenal Ladies
- Birmingham Ladies
- Liverpool Ladies
- Fulham Ladies
- Bristol City Ladies
- Doncaster Rovers Belles.

getting involved

If you're bored of trudging away on a treadmill at the gym, perhaps footie might be a more appealing form of exercise.

It'll help you get fit (it burns around 600 calories an hour), you can enjoy participating in a competitive team atmosphere, make some good mates along the way and, if you like that sort of thing, get in a big communal bath with other naked people of the same sex. Plus it's cheap to get involved – one of the reasons why football is enjoyed around the world is because the equipment needed is so basic. You'll only need football boots and shinpads (they're very necessary if you're thinking of wearing a mini skirt later in the week, but cheap), and when joining a team they will have a kit that you may have to contribute to, but that's it. And you never know, your man might fancy you all the more if you can hold your own in the park during a Sunday morning kickabout with his mates.

To get involved, get in touch with your country's football association (contacts below) and they'll be able to put you onto loads of teams in your area who are crying out for more players. For example, by visiting www.thefa.com/women, you can download a document listing the contact names and numbers of all the women's football coordinators from every county in England.

FURTHER CONTACTS

Wales: FAW Football in the Community Trust, Curran Road, Cardiff. Tel: 02920 223373 or email: fawtrust@easynet.co.uk

Scotland: Scottish Women's Football Association, Hampden Park, Glasgow.
Tel: 0141 616 6091 or email: swfa@supanet.com

N Ireland: Irish Football Association, 20 Windsor Avenue, Belfast. Tel: 028 90 669458

When you enrol with a women's club you can typically expect to spend half of the allotted time training (fitness, followed by skills) and the other half actually playing the game – except on match days, obviously. Then, after a quick scrub, you'll more than likely all trot off to the pub where you'll put back on all the weight you've just worked off by drinking half a dozen pints of fizzy brown stuff.

basic skills

Even if the last time you kicked a ball was when you were mucking about with your brother and still wearing pinafore dresses, your local women's team will still be pleased to see you. You might want to learn three key skills before you go though...

passing

Hit the ball with the side of your foot rather than the toe – this will offer you more control. You need to use your whole body to pass the ball properly. If you're right-footed, put your left foot out to one side of the ball and kick 'through' it. Don't forget to use your arms for balance, and keep your eyes on the ball if you don't want to end up on your bum on the deck with everyone laughing at you. You should aim to make contact with the centre of the ball – this keeps it low for your team-mate to control easily.

heading

You should head the ball with your forehead, as it's the safest and most accurate part of your head to use – if a ball hits the top of your skull it will merely bounce off God knows where. Keep your mouth closed to avoid biting your tongue and don't close your eyes on impact. You need to generate power, so bend your knees, arch your back and thrust your head and body forward on contact, keeping your neck muscles tensed.

shooting

It's easy to get a bit nervous when it comes to kicking the ball in the back of the net; even Zinedine Zidane, one of the greatest ever players, gets so jumpy that he actually vomits on the pitch sometimes. The most important thing is accuracy – no matter how hard you hit the ball, you're not going to score if you don't hit the target. Aim for the corners of the goal – the top corners if possible – as they're the hardest places for a keeper to cover.

11

And finally...

how to deal with defeat...

... because it's something you're just going to have to get used to, whichever team you support.

Of all the 92 sides in the football league, just one has had what could be called a perfect season in recent history, and that was Manchester United, who won the Premier League, the FA Cup and the Champions League in 1999. Even Arsenal fans, whose team went a record 49 Premiership games unbeaten in the 2003–4 season, had to taste the bitter pill of defeat when it came to their performances in Europe. No team plays perfect football and none guarantee success year in, year out – just look at Liverpool: they won pretty much every competition going in the 1970s and 1980s and now they're, well, struggling is the polite adjective.

The only way to ensure you get to celebrate winning the league every year is to see how the season pans out and then pledge your allegiance to whoever looks like winning it – but as you'll hopefully now appreciate, that sort of thing is just not done. Nope, no matter how bad it gets for your troupe of performing ball boys, you've got to stick with them through thick and thin. And, if your team is perpetually propping up the bottom of one of the lower league tables, there'll be a lot of thin.

Not that any fan would admit it, of course, but some derive a masochistic pleasure from watching their team lose again and again. It gives them something to rail against, a cause to fight for. If you find yourself taking this approach, there are plenty of outlets for your frustration. Moaning about your club in the pub should be top of your list, as it'll open up conversations with men. Bitter, sad men who drown their footballing woes with gallons of fizzy brown booze, but men nonetheless.

Radio phone-ins offer further opportunities for spleen-venting (Radio Five Live's 606 programme on Saturday evenings is particularly good, and Talk Sport should be renamed Moan Sport, such is its fondness for constantly putting despondent football fans on air). If things get really bad though, you can always get involved with the supporters' club – they're good at coordinating boardroom protests, sit-ins and terrace-based displays of dissatisfaction such as poster campaigns demanding the removal of certain members of the team/board.

However, the happiest football fans simply enjoy the good moments when they come along rather than getting bogged down by the misery of defeat. Your team mightn't have a realistic chance of winning the Premiership, but they might just be able to beat their local rivals, or they could always scrape a higher position in the league than they've ever reached before. Every goal your boys score should be a cause for celebration; if they actually win, raise a glass to them in the pub that night; and if, just if, they come away from a season with a sparkly piece of silverware, then you can treat yourself to that expensive pair of shoes you've had your eye on for months.

And what if they don't score at all, lose every match they play and get relegated? Well, as every fan knows, there's always next season...

Glossary

All the technical stuff should have been covered in the book, but here are some words, names and terms used that you may not be familiar with…

Armchair fan
A football supporter who doesn't actually go and watch live games, preferring instead to follow the sport from the comfort of his or her own front room.

AK47
A machine gun. We're not sure why we used this in the book, but it's in there somewhere.

Caca
Spanish for poo. 'Caca de la vaca' however, rhymes, rolls off the tongue really satisfyingly and means cow poo. But you don't really need to know that.

Cap
Not a form of contraception in this instance, caps are what players earn every time they play for their country. They actually do get given little embroidered hats. Thinking about it, if the players wore them, they could indeed be an effective form of contraception as they'd never get their end away.

Cross
A heck of a lot of goals come from crosses. They happen when a winger (usually) kicks the ball from the side of the pitch to a waiting striker in front of the goal.

Designer lager
A beverage, usually of European extraction and always served in a trendy bottle, favoured by baseball-hat wearing footie fans. Excessive consumption is known to bring about bouts of violence and/or woeful performances in the bedroom.

Home knits
Everyone knows what they are, but why in heaven's name do they still exist? You can buy a jumper in Asda for a fiver nowadays. It'll look rubbish, but less

rubbish than something knitted with a pair of needles by some cack-handed grandma, surely?

Livener
Also known as an opener, this is the first drink of the day and must always be consumed prior to watching a match.

Manolo Blahnik
If you're reading this entry you've probably pinched your girlfriend's book. This chap creates the finest, sexiest heels on the planet.

Penalty area
Also known as the 18 yard box or the penalty box, the penalty area extends 18 yards to each side of the goal and 18 yards in front of it. It's the bigger of the two boxes in front of the goal, not the little one – that's the goal area.

Pundits
The blazer-wearing goons who give their opinions on TV and radio. Ignore them and concentrate on the presenter of the show instead – they're often quite tasty. Well, Gary Lineker and Tim Lovejoy are alright…

Silverware
Trophies.

Stuffing
If your team's been given 'a right stuffing', it means that they've been roundly beaten. Probably by about four goals.

The Toffees
Nickname given to supporters of Everton FC. It's got something to do with a business that used to be near the ground called Mother Noblett's Toffee Shop. Or maybe it's about Everton Mints, they've got toffee in them, haven't they?

Toon Army
Nickname given to the supporters of Newcastle United FC. It's thought that they're so called because of the way Geordies pronounce the word 'town'. But then, Newcastle's a city…

The Treble
The FA Cup, the Premiership and the Champions League. Winning all three in one season is what every team's striving for.

Index